LUCIUS ANNAEUS SENECA

ON BENEFITS

THE BIG NEST

THE BIG NEST

LONDON · NEW YORK · TORONTO · SAO PAULO · MOSCOW
PARIS · MADRID · BERLIN · ROME · MEXICO CITY · MUMBAI · SEOUL · DOHA
TOKYO · SYDNEY · CAPE TOWN · AUCKLAND · BEIJING

New Edition

Published by The Big Nest

This Edition first published in 2018

Copyright © 2018 The Big Nest

All Rights Reserved.

ISBN: 9781787247154

CONTENTS

PREFACE	7
BOOK I.	13
BOOK II.	29
BOOK III.	55
BOOK IV.	82
BOOK V.	112
BOOK VI.	138
BOOK VII.	170

PREFACE

Seneca, the favourite classic of the early fathers of the church and of the Middle Ages, whom Jerome, Tertullian, and Augustine speak of as "Seneca noster," who was believed to have corresponded with St. Paul, and upon whom [Footnote: On the "De Clementia," an odd subject for the man who burned Servetus alive for differing with him.] Calvin wrote a commentary, seems almost forgotten in modern times. Perhaps some of his popularity may have been due to his being supposed to be the author of those tragedies which the world has long ceased to read, but which delighted a period that preferred Euripides to Aeschylus: while casuists must have found congenial matter in an author whose fantastic cases of conscience are often worthy of Sanchez or Escobar. Yet Seneca's morality is always pure, and from him we gain, albeit at second hand, an insight into the doctrines of the Greek philosophers, Zeno, Epicurus, Chrysippus, &c., whose precepts and system of religious thought had in cultivated Roman society taken the place of the old worship of Jupiter and Quirinus.

Since Lodge's edition (fol. 1614), no complete translation of Seneca has been published in England, though Sir Roger L'Estrange wrote paraphrases of several Dialogues, which seem to have been enormously popular, running through more than sixteen editions. I think we may conjecture that Shakespeare had seen Lodge's translation, from several allusions to philosophy, to that impossible conception "the wise man," and especially from a passage in "All's Well that ends Well," which seems to breathe the very spirit of "De Beneficiis."

"'Tis pity—
That wishing well had not a body in it
Which might be felt: that we, the poorer born,

Whose baser stars do shut us up in wishes,
Might with effects of them follow our friends
And show what we alone must think; which never
Returns us thanks."

"All's Well that ends Well," Act i. sc. 1.

Though, if this will not fit the supposed date of that play, he may have taken the idea from "The Woorke of Lucius Annaeus Seneca concerning Benefyting, that is too say, the dooing, receyving, and requyting of good turnes, translated out of Latin by A. Golding. J. Day, London, 1578." And even during the Restoration, Pepys's ideal of virtuous and lettered seclusion is a country house in whose garden he might sit on summer afternoons with his friend, Sir W. Coventry, "it maybe, to read a chapter of Seneca." In sharp contrast to this is Vahlen's preface to the minor Dialogues, which he edited after the death of his friend Koch, who had begun that work, in which he remarks that "he has read much of this writer, in order to perfect his knowledge of Latin, for otherwise he neither admires his artificial subtleties of thought, nor his childish mannerisms of style" (Vahlen, preface, p. v., ed. 1879, Jena).

Yet by the student of the history of Rome under the Caesars, Seneca is not to be neglected, because, whatever may be thought of the intrinsic merit of his speculations, he represents, more perhaps even than Tacitus, the intellectual characteristics of his age, and the tone of society in Rome—nor could we well spare the gossiping stories which we find imbedded in his graver dissertations. The following extract from Dean Merivale's "History of the Romans under the Empire" will show the estimate of him which has been formed by that accomplished writer:—

"At Rome, we, have no reason, to suppose that Christianity was only the refuge of the afflicted and miserable; rather, if we may lay any stress on the documents above referred to, it was first embraced by persons in a certain grade of comfort and respectability; by persons approaching to what we should call the MIDDLE CLASSES in their condition, their education, and their moral views. Of this class Seneca himself was the idol, the oracle; he was, so to speak, the favourite preacher of the more intelligent and humane disciples of nature and virtue. Now the writings of Seneca show, in their way, a real anxiety among this class to raise the moral tone of mankind around them; a spirit of reform, a zeal for the conversion of souls, which, though it never rose, indeed, under the teaching of the philosophers, to boiling heat, still simmered with genial warmth on the surface of society. Far different as was their social standing-point, far different as were the foundations and the presumed sanctions of their teaching respectively, Seneca and St. Paul were both moral reformers; both, be it said with reverence, were fellow-workers in the cause of humanity, though the Christian could look beyond the proximate aims of morality and prepare men for a final development on which the Stoic could not venture to gaze. Hence there is so much in their principles, so much even in their language, which agrees together, so that the one has been thought, though it must be allowed without adequate reason, to have borrowed directly from the other. [Footnote: It is hardly necessary to refer to the pretended letters between St. Paul and Seneca. Besides the evidence from style, some of the dates they contain are quite sufficient to condemn them as clumsy forgeries. They are mentioned, but with no expression of belief in their genuineness, by Jerome and Augustine. See Jones, "On the Canon," ii. 80.]

"But the philosopher, be it remembered, discoursed to a large and not inattentive audience, and surely the soil was not all unfruitful on which his seed was scattered when he proclaimed that God dwells not in temples of wood and stone, nor wants the ministrations of human hands;[Footnote: Sen., Ep. 95, and in Lactantius, Inst. vi.] that He has no delight in the blood of victims:[Footnote: Ep. 116: "Colitur Deus non tauris sed pia et recta voluntate."] that He is near to all His creatures:[Footnote: Ep. 41, 73.] that His Spirit resides in men's hearts:[Footnote: Ep. 46: "Sacer intra nos spiritus sedet."] that all men are truly His offspring:[Footnote: "De Prov," i.] that we are members of one body, which is God or Nature;[Footnote: Ep. 93, 95: "Membra sumus magni corporis."] that men must believe in God before they can approach Him:[Footnote: Ep. 95: "Primus Deorum cultus est Deos credere."] that the true service of God is to be like unto Him:[Footnote: Ep. 95: "Satis coluit quisquis imitatus est."] that all men have sinned, and none performed all the works of the law:[Footnote: Sen. de Ira. i. 14; ii. 27: "Quis est iste qui se profitetur omnibus legibus innocentem?"] that God is no respecter of nations, ranks, or conditions, but all, barbarian and Roman, bond and free, are alike under His all-seeing Providence.[Footnote: "De Benef.," iii. 18: "Virtus omnes admittit, libertinos, servos, reges." These and many other passages are collected by Champagny, ii. 546, after Fabricius and others, and compared with well-known texts of Scripture. The version of the Vulgate shows a great deal of verbal correspondence. M. Troplong remarks, after De Maistre, that Seneca has written a fine book on Providence, for which there was not even a name at Rome in the time of Cicero.—"L'Influence du Christianisme," &c., i., ch. 4.]

"St. Paul enjoined submission and obedience even to the tyranny of Nero, and Seneca fosters no ideas subversive of political subjection. Endurance is the paramount virtue of the Stoic. To forms of government the wise man was wholly indifferent; they were among the external circumstances above which his spirit soared in serene self-contemplation. We trace in Seneca no yearning for a restoration of political freedom, nor does he even point to the senate, after the manner of the patriots of the day, as a legitimate check to the autocracy of the despot. The only mode, in his view, of tempering tyranny is to educate the tyrant himself in virtue. His was the self-denial of the Christians, but without their anticipated compensation. It seems impossible to doubt that in his highest flights of rhetoric—and no man ever recommended the unattainable with a finer grace—Seneca must have felt that he was labouring to build up a house without foundations; that his system, as Caius said of his style, was sand without lime. He was surely not unconscious of the inconsistency of his own position, as a public man and a minister, with the theories to which he had wedded himself; and of the impossibility of preserving in it the purity of his character as a philosopher or a man. He was aware that in the existing state of society at Rome, wealth was necessary to men high in station; wealth alone could retain influence, and a poor minister became at once contemptible. The distributor of the Imperial favours must have his banquets, his receptions, his slaves and freedmen; he must possess the means of attracting if not of bribing; he must not seem too virtuous, too austere, among an evil generation; in order to do good at all he must swim with the stream, however polluted it might be. All this inconsistency Seneca must have contemplated without blenching; and there is something touching in the serenity he preserved amidst the conflict that must have perpetually raged between his natural sense and his acquired principles. Both Cicero and Seneca were men of many weaknesses, and we remark them the more because both were pretenders to unusual strength of character; but while Cicero lapsed into political errors, Seneca cannot be absolved of actual crime. Nevertheless, if we may compare the greatest masters of Roman wisdom together, the Stoic will appear, I think, the more earnest of the two, the more anxious to do his duty for its own sake, the more sensible of the claims of mankind upon him for such precepts of virtuous living as he had to give. In an age of unbelief and compromise he taught that Truth was positive and Virtue objective. He conceived, what never entered Cicero's mind, the idea of improving his fellow-creatures; he had, what Cicero had not, a heart for conversion to Christianity."

To this eloquent account of Seneca's position and of the tendency of his writings I have nothing to add. The main particulars of his life, his Spanish extraction (like that of Lacan and Martial), his father's treatises on Rhetoric, his mother Helvia, his brothers, his wealth, his exile in Corsica, his outrageous flattery of Claudius and his satiric poem on his death—"The Vision of Judgment," Merivale calls it, after Lord Byron—his position as Nero's tutor, and his death, worthy at once of a Roman and a Stoic, by the orders of that tyrant, may be read of in "The History of the Romans under the Empire," or in the article "Seneca" in the "Dictionary of Classical Biography," and need not be reproduced here: but I cannot resist pointing out how entirely Grote's view of the "Sophists" as a sort of established clergy, and Seneca's account of the various sects of philosophers as representing the religious thought of the time, is illustrated by his anecdote of Julia Augusta, the mother of Tiberius, better known to English readers as Livia the wife of Augustus, who in her first agony of grief at the loss of her first husband applied to his Greek philosopher, Areus, as to a kind of domestic chaplain, for spiritual consolation. ("Ad Marciam de Consolatione," ch. iv.)

I take this opportunity of expressing my gratitude to the Rev. J. E. B. Mayor, Professor of Latin in the University of Cambridge, for his kindness in finding time among his many and important literary labours for reading and correcting the proofs of this work.

The text which I have followed for De Beneficiis is that of Gertz, Berlin (1876.).

AUBREY STEWART
London, March, 1887.

BOOK I.

I.

Among the numerous faults of those who pass their lives recklessly and without due reflexion, my good friend Liberalis, I should say that there is hardly any one so hurtful to society as this, that we neither know how to bestow or how to receive a benefit. It follows from this that benefits are badly invested, and become bad debts: in these cases it is too late to complain of their not being returned, for they were thrown away when we bestowed them. Nor need we wonder that while the greatest vices are common, none is more common than ingratitude: for this I see is brought about by various causes. The first of these is, that we do not choose worthy persons upon whom to bestow our bounty, but although when we are about to lend money we first make a careful enquiry into the means and habits of life of our debtor, and avoid sowing seed in a worn-out or unfruitful soil, yet without any discrimination we scatter our benefits at random rather than bestow them. It is hard to say whether it is more dishonourable for the receiver to disown a benefit, or for the giver to demand a return of it: for a benefit is a loan, the repayment of which depends merely upon the good feeling of the debtor. To misuse a benefit like a spendthrift is most shameful, because we do not need our wealth but only our intention to set us free from the obligation of it; for a benefit is repaid by being acknowledged. Yet while they are to blame who do not even show so much gratitude as to acknowledge their debt, we ourselves are to blame no less. We find many men ungrateful, yet we make more men so, because at one time we harshly and reproachfully demand some return for our bounty, at another we are fickle and regret what we have given, at another we are peevish and apt to find fault with trifles. By acting thus we destroy all sense of gratitude, not only after we have given anything, but while we are in the act of giving it. Who has ever thought it enough to be asked for anything in an off-hand manner, or to be asked only once? Who, when he suspected that he was going to be asked for any thing, has not frowned, turned away his face, pretended to be busy, or purposely talked without ceasing, in order not to give his suitor a chance of preferring his request, and avoided by various tricks having to help his friend in his pressing need? and when driven into a corner, has not either put the matter off, that is, given a cowardly refusal, or promised his help ungraciously, with a wry face, and with unkind words, of which he seemed to grudge the utterance. Yet no one is glad to owe what he has not so much received from his benefactor, as wrung out of him. Who can be grateful for what has been disdainfully flung to him, or angrily cast at him, or been given him out of weariness, to avoid further trouble? No one need expect any return from those whom he has tired out with delays, or sickened with expectation. A benefit is received in the same temper in which it is given, and ought not, therefore, to be given carelessly, for a man thanks himself for that which he receives without the knowledge of the giver. Neither ought we to give after long delay, because in all good offices the will of the giver counts for much, and he who gives tardily must long have been unwilling to give at all. Nor, assuredly, ought we to give in offensive manner, because human nature is so constituted that insults sink deeper than kindnesses; the remembrance of the latter soon passes away, while that of the former is treasured in the memory; so what can a man expect who insults while he obliges? All the gratitude which he deserves is to be forgiven for helping us. On the other hand, the number of the ungrateful ought not to deter us from earning men's gratitude; for, in the first place, their number is increased by our own acts. Secondly, the sacrilege and indifference to religion of some men does not prevent even the immortal gods from continuing to shower their benefits upon us: for they act according to their divine nature and help all alike, among them even those who so ill appreciate their bounty. Let us take them for our guides as far as the weakness of our mortal nature permits; let us bestow benefits, not put them out at interest. The man who while he gives thinks of what he will get in return, deserves to be deceived. But what if the benefit turns out ill? Why, our wives and our children often disappoint our hopes, yet we marry—and bring up children, and are so obstinate in the face of experience that we fight after we have been beaten, and put to sea after we have been shipwrecked. How much more constancy ought we to show in bestowing benefits! If a man does not bestow benefits because he has not received any, he must have bestowed them in order to receive them in return, and he justifies ingratitude, whose disgrace lies in not returning benefits when able to do so. How many are there who are unworthy of the light of day? and nevertheless the sun rises. How many complain because they have been born? yet Nature is ever renewing our race, and even suffers men to live who wish that they had never lived. It is the property of a great and good mind to covet, not the fruit of good deeds, but good deeds themselves, and to seek for a good man even after having met with bad men. If there were no rogues, what glory would there be in doing good to many? As it is, virtue consists in bestowing benefits for which we are not certain of meeting with any return, but whose fruit is at once enjoyed by noble minds. So little influence ought this to have in restraining us from doing good actions, that even though I were denied the hope of meeting with a grateful man, yet the fear of not having my benefits returned would not prevent my bestowing them, because he who does not give, forestalls the vice of him who is ungrateful. I will explain what I mean. He who does not repay a benefit, sins more, but he who does not bestow one, sins earlier.

"If thou at random dost thy bounties waste,

Much must be lost, for one that's rightly placed."

II. In the former verse you may blame two things, for one should not cast them at random, and it is not right to waste anything, much less benefits; for unless they be given with judgement, they cease to be benefits, and, may be called by any other name you please. The meaning of the latter verse is admirable, that one benefit rightly bestowed makes amends for the loss of many that have been lost. See, I pray you, whether it be not truer and more worthy of the glory of the giver, that we should encourage him to give, even though none of his gifts should be worthily placed. "Much must be lost." Nothing is lost because he who loses had counted the cost before. The book-keeping of benefits is simple: it is all expenditure; if any one returns it, that is clear gain; if he does not return it, it is not lost, I gave it for the sake of giving. No one writes down his gifts in a ledger, or like a grasping creditor demands repayment to the day and hour. A good man never thinks of such matters, unless reminded of them by some one returning his gifts; otherwise they become like debts owing to him. It is a base usury to regard a benefit as an investment. Whatever may have been the result of your former benefits, persevere in bestowing others upon other men; they will be all the better placed in the hands of the ungrateful, whom shame, or a favourable opportunity, or imitation of others may some day cause to be grateful. Do not grow weary, perform your duty, and act as becomes a good man. Help one man with money, another with credit, another with your favour; this man with good advice, that one with sound maxims. Even wild beasts feel kindness, nor is there any animal so savage that good treatment will not tame it and win love from it. The mouths of lions are handled by their keepers with impunity; to obtain their food fierce elephants become as docile as slaves: so that constant unceasing kindness wins the hearts even of creatures who, by their nature, cannot comprehend or weigh the value of a benefit. Is a man ungrateful for one benefit? perhaps he will not be so after receiving a second. Has he forgotten two kindnesses? perhaps by a third he may be brought to remember the former ones also.

III. He who is quick to believe that he has thrown away his benefits, does really throw them away; but he who presses on and adds new benefits to his former ones, forces out gratitude even from a hard and forgetful breast. In the face of many kindnesses, your friend will not dare to raise his eyes; let him see you whithersoever he turns himself to escape from his remembrance of you; encircle him with your benefits. As for the power and property of these, I will explain it to you if first you will allow me to glance at a matter which does not belong to our subject, as to why the Graces are three in number, why they are sisters, why hand in hand, and why they are smiling and young, with a loose and transparent dress. Some writers think that there is one who bestows a benefit, one who receives it, and a third who returns it; others say that they represent the three sorts of benefactors, those who bestow, those who repay, and those who both receive and repay them. But take whichever you please to be true; what will this knowledge profit us? What is the meaning of this dance of sisters in a circle, hand in hand? It means that the course of a benefit is from hand to hand, back to the giver; that the beauty of the whole chain is lost if a single link fails, and that it is fairest when it proceeds in unbroken regular order. In the dance there is one, esteemed beyond the others, who represents the givers of benefits. Their faces are cheerful, as those of men who give or receive benefits are wont to be. They are young, because the memory of benefits ought not to grow old. They are virgins, because benefits are pure and untainted, and held holy by all; in benefits there should be no strict or binding conditions, therefore the Graces wear loose flowing tunics, which are transparent, because benefits love to be seen. People who are not under the influence of Greek literature may say that all this is a matter of course; but there can be no one who would think that the names which Hesiod has given them bear upon our subject. He named the eldest Aglaia, the middle one Euphrosyne, the third Thalia. Every one, according to his own ideas, twists the meaning of these names, trying to reconcile them with some system, though Hesiod merely gave his maidens their names from his own fancy. So Homer altered the name of one of them, naming her Pasithea, and betrothed her to a husband, in order that you may know that they are not vestal virgins. [Footnote: i.e. not vowed to chastity.]

I could find another poet, in whose writings they are girded, and wear thick or embroidered Phrygian robes. Mercury stands with them for the same reason, not because argument or eloquence commends benefits, but because the painter chose to do so. Also Chrysippus, that man of piercing intellect who saw to the very bottom of truth, who speaks only to the point, and makes use of no more words than are necessary to express his meaning, fills his whole treatise with these puerilities, insomuch that he says but very little about the duties of giving, receiving, and returning a benefit, and has not so much inserted fables among these subjects, as he has inserted these subjects among a mass of fables. For, not to mention what Hecaton borrows from him, Chrysippus tells us that the three Graces are the daughters of Jupiter and Eurynome, that they are younger than the Hours, and rather more beautiful, and that on that account they are assigned as companions to Venus. He also thinks that the name of their mother bears upon the subject, and that she is named Eurynome because to distribute benefits requires a wide inheritance; as if the mother usually received her name after her daughters, or as if the names given by poets were true. In truth, just as with a 'nomenclator' audacity supplies the place of memory, and he invents a name for every one whose name he cannot recollect, so the poets think that it is of no importance to speak the truth, but are either forced by the exigencies of metre, or attracted by sweetness of sound, into calling every one by whatever name runs neatly into verse. Nor do they suffer for it if they introduce another name into the list, for the next poet makes them bear what name he pleases. That you may know that this is so, for instance Thalia, our present subject of discourse, is one of the Graces in Hesiod's poems, while in those of Homer she is one of the Muses.

IV. But lest I should do the very thing which I am blaming, I will pass over all these matters, which are so far from the subject that they are not even connected with it. Only do you protect me, if any one attacks me for putting down Chrysippus, who, by Hercules, was a great man, but yet a Greek, whose intellect, too sharply pointed, is often bent and turned back upon itself; even when it seems to be in earnest it only pricks, but does not pierce. Here, however, what occasion is there for subtlety? We are to speak of benefits, and to define a matter which is the chief bond of human society; we are to lay down a rule of life, such that neither careless openhandedness may commend itself to us under the guise of goodness of heart, and yet that our circumspection, while it moderates, may not quench our generosity, a quality in which we ought neither to exceed nor to fall short. Men must be taught to be willing to give, willing to receive, willing to return; and to place before themselves the high aim, not merely of equalling, but even of surpassing those to whom they are indebted, both in good offices and in good feeling; because the man whose duty it is to repay, can never do so unless he outdoes his benefactor; [Footnote: That is, he never comes up to his benefactor unless he leaves him behind: he can only make a dead heat of it by getting a start.] the one class must be taught to look for no return, the other to feel deeper gratitude. In this noblest of contests to outdo benefits by benefits, Chrysippus encourages us by bidding us beware lest, as the Graces are the daughters of Jupiter, to act ungratefully may not be a sin against them, and may not wrong those beauteous maidens. Do thou teach me how I may bestow more good things, and be more grateful to those who have earned my gratitude, and how the minds of both parties may vie with one another, the giver in forgetting, the receiver in remembering his debt. As for those other follies, let them be left to the poets, whose purpose is merely to charm the ear and to weave a pleasing story; but let those who wish to purify men's minds, to retain honour in their dealings, and to imprint on their minds gratitude for kindnesses, let them speak in sober earnest and act with all their strength; unless you imagine, perchance, that by such flippant and mythical talk, and such old wives' reasoning, it is possible for us to prevent that most ruinous consummation, the repudiation of benefits.

V. However, while I pass over what is futile and irrelevant I must point out that the first thing which we have to learn is, what we owe in return for a benefit received. One man says that he owes the money which he has received, another that he owes a consulship, a priesthood, a province, and so on. These, however, are but the outward signs of kindnesses, not the kindnesses themselves. A benefit is not to be felt and handled, it is a thing which exists only in the mind. There is a great difference between the subject-matter of a benefit, and the benefit itself. Wherefore neither gold, nor silver, nor any of those things which are most highly esteemed, are benefits, but the benefit lies in the goodwill of him who gives them. The ignorant take notice only of that which comes before their eyes, and which can be owned and passed from hand to hand, while they disregard that which gives these things their value. The things which we hold in our hands, which we see with our eyes, and which our avarice hugs, are transitory, they may be taken from us by ill luck or by violence; but a kindness lasts even after the loss of that by means of which it was bestowed; for it is a good deed, which no violence can undo. For instance, suppose that I ransomed a friend from pirates, but another pirate has caught him and thrown him into prison. The pirate has not robbed him of my benefit, but has only robbed him of the enjoyment of it. Or suppose that I have saved a man's children from a shipwreck or a fire, and that afterwards disease or accident has carried them off; even when they are no more, the kindness which was done by means of them remains. All those things, therefore, which improperly assume the name of benefits, are means by which kindly feeling manifests itself. In other cases also, we find a distinction between the visible symbol and the matter itself, as when a general bestows collars of gold, or civic or mural crowns upon any one. What value has the crown in itself? or the purple-bordered robe? or the fasces? or the judgment-seat and car of triumph? None of these things is in itself an honour, but is an emblem of honour. In like manner, that which is seen is not a benefit—it is but the trace and mark of a benefit.

VI. What, then, is a benefit? It is the art of doing a kindness which both bestows pleasure and gains it by bestowing it, and which does its office by natural and spontaneous impulse. It is not, therefore, the thing which is done or given, but the spirit in which it is done or given, that must be considered, because a benefit exists, not in that which is done or given, but in the mind of the doer or giver. How great the distinction between them is, you may perceive from this, that while a benefit is necessarily good, yet that which is done or given is neither good nor bad. The spirit in which they are given can exalt small things, can glorify mean ones, and can discredit great and precious ones; the objects themselves which are sought after have a neutral nature, neither good nor bad; all depends upon the direction given them by the guiding spirit from which things receive their shape. That which is paid or handed over is not the benefit itself, just as the honour which we pay to the gods lies not in the victims themselves, although they be fat and glittering with gold, [Footnote: Alluding to the practice of gilding the horns of the victims.] but in the pure and holy feelings of the worshippers.

Thus good men are religious, though their offering be meal and their vessels of earthenware; whilst bad men will not escape from their impiety, though they pour the blood of many victims upon the altars.

VII. If benefits consisted of things, and not of the wish to benefit, then the more things we received the greater the benefit would be. But this is not true, for sometimes we feel more gratitude to one who gives us trifles nobly, who, like Virgil's poor old soldier, "holds himself as rich as kings," if he has given us ever so little with a good will a man who forgets his own need when he sees mine, who has not only a wish but a longing to help, who thinks that he receives a benefit when he bestows one, who gives as though he would receive no return, receives a repayment as though he had originally given nothing, and who watches for and seizes an opportunity of being useful. On the other hand, as I said before, those gifts which are hardly wrung from the giver, or which drop unheeded from his hands, claim no gratitude from us, however great they may appear and may be. We prize much more what comes from a willing hand, than what comes from a full one. This man has given me but little, yet more he could not afford, while what that one has given is much indeed, but he hesitated, he put it off, he grumbled when he gave it, he gave it haughtily, or he proclaimed it aloud, and did it to please others, not to please the person to whom he gave it; he offered it to his own pride, not to me.

VIII. As the pupils of Socrates, each in proportion to his means, gave him large presents, Aeschines, a poor pupil, said, "I can find nothing to give you which is worthy of you; I feel my poverty in this respect alone. Therefore I present you with the only thing I possess, myself. I pray that you may take this my present, such as it is, in good part, and may remember that the others, although they gave you much, yet left for themselves more than they gave." Socrates answered, "Surely you have bestowed a great present upon me, unless perchance you set a small value upon yourself. I will accordingly take pains to restore you to yourself a better man than when I received you." By this present Aeschines outdid Alcibiades, whose mind was as great as his Wealth, and all the splendour of the most wealthy youths of Athens.

IX. You see how the mind even in the straitest circumstances finds the means of generosity. Aeschines seems to me to have said, "Fortune, it is in vain that you have made me poor; in spite of this I will find a worthy present for this man. Since I can give him nothing of yours, I will give him something of my own." Nor need you suppose that he held himself cheap; he made himself his own price. By a stroke of genius this youth discovered a means of presenting Socrates to himself. We must not consider how great presents are, but in what spirit they are given.

A rich man is well spoken of if he is clever enough to render himself easy of access to men of immoderate ambition, and although he intends to do nothing to help them, yet encourages their unconscionable hopes; but he is thought the worse of if he be sharp of tongue, sour in appearance, and displays his wealth in an invidious fashion. For men respect and yet loathe a fortunate man, and hate him for doing what, if they had the chance, they would do themselves.

* * * * * * *

Men nowadays no longer secretly, but openly outrage the wives of others, and allow to others access to their own wives. A match is thought countrified, uncivilized, in bad style, and to be protested against by all matrons, if the husband should forbid his wife to appear in public in a litter, and to be carried about exposed to the gaze of all observers. If a man has not made himself notorious by a LIAISON with some mistress, if he does not pay an annuity to some one else's wife, married women speak of him as a poor-spirited creature, a man given to low vice, a lover of servant girls. Soon adultery becomes the most respectable form of marriage, and widowhood and celibacy are commonly practised. No one takes a wife unless he takes her away from some one else. Now men vie with one another in wasting what they have stolen, and in collecting together what they have wasted with the keenest avarice; they become utterly reckless, scorn poverty in others, fear personal injury more than anything else, break the peace by their riots, and by violence and terror domineer over those who are weaker than themselves. No wonder that they plunder provinces and offer the seat of judgment for sale, knocking it down after an auction to the highest bidder, since it is the law of nations that you may sell what you have bought.

X. However, my enthusiasm has carried me further than I intended, the subject being an inviting one. Let me, then, end by pointing out that the disgrace of these crimes does not belong especially to our own time. Our ancestors before us have lamented, and our children after us will lament, as we do, the ruin, of morality, the prevalence of vice, and the gradual deterioration of mankind; yet these things are really stationary, only moved slightly to and fro like the waves which at one time a rising tide washes further over the land, and at another an ebbing one restrains within a lower water mark. At one time the chief vice will be adultery, and licentiousness will exceed all bounds; at another time a rage for feasting will be in vogue, and men will waste their inheritance in the most shameful of all ways, by the kitchen; at another, excessive care for the body, and a devotion to personal beauty which implies ugliness of mind; at another time, injudiciously granted liberty will show itself in wanton recklessness and defiance of authority; sometimes there will be a reign of cruelty both in public and private, and the madness of the civil wars will come upon us, which destroy all that is holy and inviolable. Sometimes even drunkenness will be held in honour, and it will be a virtue to swallow most wine. Vices do not lie in wait for us in one place alone, but hover around us in changeful forms, sometimes even at variance one with another, so that in turn they win and lose the field; yet we shall always be obliged to pronounce the same verdict upon ourselves, that we are and always were evil, and, I unwillingly add, that we always shall be. There always will be homicides, tyrants, thieves, adulterers, ravishers, sacrilegious, traitors: worse than all these is the ungrateful man, except we consider that all these crimes flow from ingratitude, without which hardly any great wickedness has ever grown to full stature. Be sure that you guard against this as the greatest of crimes in yourself, but pardon it as the least of crimes in another. For all the injury which you suffer is this: you have lost the subject-matter of a benefit, not the benefit itself, for you possess unimpaired the best part of it, in that you have given it. Though we ought to be careful to bestow our benefits by preference upon those who are likely to show us gratitude for them, yet we must sometimes do what we have little hope will turn out well, and bestow benefits upon those who we not only think will prove ungrateful, but who we know have been so. For instance, if I should be able to save a man's children from a great danger with no risk to myself, I should not hesitate to do so. If a man be worthy I would defend him even with my blood, and would share his perils; if he be unworthy, and yet by merely crying for help I can rescue him from robbers, I would without reluctance raise the shout which would save a fellow-creature.

XI. The next point to be defined is, what kind of benefits are to be given, and in what manner. First let us give what is necessary, next what is useful, and then what is pleasant, provided that they be lasting. We must begin with what is necessary, for those things which support life affect the mind very differently from, those which adorn and improve it. A man may be nice, and hard to please, in things which he can easily do without, of which he can say, "Take them back; I do not want them, I am satisfied with what I have." Sometimes, we wish not only to, return what we have received, but even to throw it away. Of necessary things, the first class consists of things without which we cannot live; the second, of things without which we ought not to live; and the third, of things without which we should not care to live. The first class are, to be saved from the hands of the enemy, from the anger of tyrants, from proscription, and the various other perils which beset human life. By averting any one of these, we shall earn gratitude proportionate to the greatness of the danger, for when men think of the greatness of the misery from which they have been saved, the terror which they have gone through enhances the value of our services. Yet we ought not to delay rescuing any one longer than we are obliged, solely in order to make his fears add weight to our services. Next come those things without which we can indeed live, but in such a manner that it would be better to die, such as liberty, chastity, or a good conscience. After these are what we have come to hold dear by connexion and relationship and long use and custom, such as our wives and children, our household gods, and so on, to which the mind so firmly attaches itself that separation from them seems worse than death.

After these come useful things, which form a very wide and varied class; in which will be money, not in excess, but enough for living in a moderate style; public office, and, for the ambitious, due advancement to higher posts; for nothing can be more useful to a man than to be placed in a position in which he can benefit himself. All benefits beyond these are superfluous, and are likely to spoil those who receive them. In giving these we must be careful to make them acceptable by giving them at the appropriate time, or by giving things which are not common, but such as few people possess, or at any rate few possess in our times; or again, by giving things in such a manner, that though not naturally valuable, they become so by the time and place at which they are given. We must reflect what present will produce the most pleasure, what will most frequently come under the notice of the possessor of it, so that whenever he is with it he may be with us also; and in all cases we must be careful not to send useless presents, such as hunting weapons to a woman or old man, or books to a rustic, or nets to catch wild animals to a quiet literary man. On the other hand, we ought to be careful, while we wish to send what will please, that we do not send what will insultingly remind our friends of their failings, as, for example, if we send wine to a hard drinker or drugs to an invalid, for a present which contains an allusion to the shortcomings of the receiver, becomes an outrage.

XII. If we have a free choice as to what to give, we should above all choose lasting presents, in order that our gift may endure as long as possible; for few are so grateful as to think of what they have received, even when they do not see it. Even the ungrateful remember us by our gifts, when they are always in their sight and do not allow themselves to be forgotten, but constantly obtrude and stamp upon the mind the memory of the giver. As we never ought to remind men of what we have given them, we ought all the more to choose presents that will be permanent; for the things themselves will prevent the remembrance of the giver from fading away. I would more willingly give a present of plate than of coined money, and would more willingly give statues than clothes or other things which are soon worn out. Few remain grateful after the present is gone: many more remember their presents only while they make use of them. If possible, I should like my present not to be consumed; let it remain in existence, let it stick to my friend and share his life. No one is so foolish as to need to be told not to send gladiators or wild beasts to one who has just given a public show, or not to send summer clothing in winter time, or winter clothing in summer. Common sense must guide our benefits; we must consider the time and the place, and the character of the receiver, which are the weights in the scale, which cause our gifts to be well or ill received. How far more acceptable a present is, if we give a man what he has not, than if we give him what he has plenty of! if we give him what he has long been searching for in vain, rather than what he sees everywhere! Let us make presents of things which are rare and scarce rather than costly, things which even a rich man will be glad of, just as common fruits, such as we tire of after a few days, please us if they have ripened before the usual season. People will also esteem things which no one else has given to them, or which we have given to no one else.

XIII. When the conquest of the East had flattered Alexander

of Macedon into believing himself to be more than man, the people of Corinth sent an embassy to congratulate him, and presented him with the franchise of their city. When Alexander smiled at this form of courtesy, one of the ambassadors said, "We have never enrolled any stranger among our citizens except Hercules and yourself." Alexander willingly accepted the proffered honour, invited the ambassadors to his table, and showed them other courtesies. He did not think of who offered the citizenship, but to whom they had granted it; and being altogether the slave of glory, though he knew neither its true nature or its limits, had followed in the footsteps of Hercules and Bacchus, and had not even stayed his march where they ceased; so that he glanced aside from the givers of this honour to him with whom he shared it, and fancied that the heaven to which his vanity aspired was indeed opening before him when he was made equal to Hercules. In what indeed did that frantic youth, whose only merit was his lucky audacity, resemble Hercules? Hercules conquered nothing for himself; he travelled throughout the world, not coveting for himself but liberating the countries which he conquered, an enemy to bad men, a defender of the good, a peacemaker both by sea and land; whereas the other was from his boyhood a brigand and desolator of nations, a pest to his friends and enemies alike, whose greatest joy was to be the terror of all mankind, forgetting that men fear not only the fiercest but also the most cowardly animals, because of their evil and venomous nature.

XIV. Let us now return to our subject. He who bestows a benefit without discrimination, gives what pleases no one; no one considers himself to be under any obligation to the landlord of a tavern, or to be the guest of any one with whom he dines in such company as to be able to say, "What civility has he shown to me? no more than he has shown to that man, whom he scarcely knows, or to that other, who is both his personal enemy and a man of infamous character. Do you suppose that he wished to do me any honour? not so, he merely wished to indulge his own vice of profusion." If you wish men to be grateful for anything, give it but seldom; no one can bear to receive what you give to all the world. Yet let no one gather from this that I wish to impose any bonds upon generosity; let her go to what lengths she will, so that she go a steady course, not at random. It is possible to bestow gifts in such a manner that each of those who receive them, although he shares them with many others, may yet feel himself to be distinguished from the common herd. Let each man have some peculiarity about his gift which may make him consider himself more highly favoured than the rest. He may say, "I received the same present that he did, but I never asked for it." "I received the same present, but mine was given me after a few days, whereas he had earned it by long service." "Others have the same present, but it was not given to them with the same courtesy and gracious words with which it was given to me." "That man got it because he asked for it; I did not ask." "That man received it as well as I, but then he could easily return it; one has great expectations from a rich man, old and childless, as he is; whereas in giving the same present to me he really gave more, because he gave it without the hope of receiving any return for it." Just as a courtesan divides her favours among many men, so that no one of her friends is without some proof of her affection, so let him who wishes his benefits to be prized consider how he may at the same time gratify many men, and nevertheless give each one of them some especial mark of favour to distinguish him from the rest.

XV. I am no advocate of slackness in giving benefits: the more and the greater they are, the more praise they will bring to the giver. Yet let them be given with discretion; for what is given carelessly and recklessly can please no one. Whoever, therefore, supposes that in giving this advice I wish to restrict benevolence and to confine it to narrower limits, entirely mistakes the object of my warning. What virtue do we admire more than benevolence? Which do we encourage more? Who ought to applaud it more than we Stoics, who preach the brotherhood of the human race? What then is it? Since no impulse of the human mind can be approved of, even though it springs from a right feeling, unless it be made into a virtue by discretion, I forbid generosity to degenerate into extravagance. It is, indeed, pleasant to receive a benefit with open arms, when reason bestows it upon the worthy, not when it is flung hither or thither thoughtlessly and at random; this alone we care to display and claim as our own. Can you call anything a benefit, if you feel ashamed to mention the person who gave it you? How far more grateful is a benefit, how far more deeply does it impress itself upon the mind, never to be forgotten, when we rejoice to think not so much of what it is, as from whom we have received it! Crispus Passienus was wont to say that some men's advice was to be preferred to their presents, some men's presents to their advice; and he added as an example, "I would rather have received advice from Augustus than a present; I would rather receive a present from Claudius than advice." I, however, think that one ought not to wish for a benefit from any man whose judgement is worthless. What then? Ought we not to receive what Claudius gives? We ought; but we ought to regard it as obtained from fortune, which may at any moment turn against us. Why do we separate this which naturally is connected? That is not a benefit, to which the best part of a benefit, that it be bestowed with judgment, is wanting: a really great sum of money, if it be given neither with discernment nor with good will, is no more a benefit than if it remained hoarded. There are, however, many things which we ought not to reject, yet for which we cannot feel indebted.

BOOK II.

I.

Let us consider, most excellent Liberalis, what still remains of the earlier part of the subject; in what way a benefit should be bestowed. I think that I can point out the shortest way to this; let us give in the way in which we ourselves should like to receive. Above all we should give willingly, quickly, and without any hesitation; a benefit commands no gratitude if it has hung for a long time in the hands of the giver, if he seems unwilling to part with it, and gives it as though he were being robbed of it. Even though some delay should intervene, let us by all means in our power strive not to seem to have been in two minds about giving it at all. To hesitate is the next thing to refusing to give, and destroys all claim to gratitude. For just as the sweetest part of a benefit is the kindly feeling of the giver, it follows that one who has by his very delay proved that he gives unwillingly, must be regarded not as having given anything, but as having been unable to keep it from an importunate suitor. Indeed, many men are made generous by want of firmness. The most acceptable benefits are those which are waiting for us to take them, which are easy to be received, and offer themselves to us, so that the only delay is caused by the modesty of the receiver. The best thing of all is to anticipate a person's wishes; the next, to follow them; the former is the better course, to be beforehand with our friends by giving them what they want before they ask us for it, for the value of a gift is much enhanced by sparing an honest man the misery of asking for it with confusion and blushes. He who gets what he asked for does not get it for nothing, for indeed, as our austere ancestors thought, nothing is so dear as that which is bought by prayers. Men would be much more modest in their petitions to heaven, if these had to be made publicly; so that even when addressing the gods, before whom we can with all honour bend our knees, we prefer to pray silently and within ourselves.

II. It is unpleasant, burdensome, and covers one with shame to have to say, "Give me." You should spare your friends, and those whom you wish to make your friends, from having to do this; however quick he may be, a man gives too late who gives what he has been asked for. We ought, therefore, to divine every man's wishes, and when we have discovered them, to set him free from the hard necessity of asking; you may be sure that a benefit which comes unasked will be delightful and will not be forgotten. If we do not succeed in anticipating our friends, let us at any rate cut them short when they ask us for anything, so that we may appear to be reminded of what we meant to do, rather than to have been asked to do it. Let us assent at once, and by our promptness make it appear that we meant to do so even before we were solicited. As in dealing with sick persons much depends upon when food is given, and plain water given at the right moment sometimes acts as a remedy, so a benefit, however slight and commonplace it may be, if it be promptly given without losing a moment of time, gains enormously in importance, and wins our gratitude more than a far more valuable present given after long waiting and deliberation. One who gives so readily must needs give with good will; he therefore gives cheerfully and shows his disposition in his countenance.

III. Many who bestow immense benefits spoil them by their silence or slowness of speech, which gives them an air of moroseness, as they say "yes" with a face which seems to say "no." How much better is it to join kind words to kind actions, and to enhance the value of our gifts by a civil and gracious commendation of them! To cure your friend of being slow to ask a favour of you, you may join to your gift the familiar rebuke, "I am angry with you for not having long ago let me know what you wanted, for having asked for it so formally, or for having made interest with a third party." "I congratulate myself that you have been pleased to make trial of me; hereafter, if you want anything, ask for it as your right; however, for this time I pardon your want of manners." By so doing you will cause him to value your friendship more highly than that, whatever it may have been, which he came to ask of you. The goodness and kindness of a benefactor never appears so great as when on leaving him one says, "I have to-day gained much; I am more pleased at finding him so kind than if I had obtained many times more of this, of which I was speaking, by some other means; I never can make any adequate return to this man for his goodness."

IV. Many, however, there are who, by harsh words and contemptuous manner, make their very kindnesses odious, for by speaking and acting disdainfully they make us sorry that they have granted our requests. Various delays also take place after we have obtained a promise; and nothing is more heartbreaking than to be forced to beg for the very thing which you already have been promised. Benefits ought to be bestowed at once, but from some persons it is easier to obtain the promise of them than to get them. One man has to be asked to remind our benefactor of his purpose; another, to bring it into effect; and thus a single present is worn away in passing through many hands, until hardly any gratitude is left for the original promiser, since whoever we are forced to solicit after the giving of the promise receives some of the gratitude which we owe to the giver. Take care, therefore, if you wish your gifts to be esteemed, that they reach those to whom they are promised entire, and, as the saying is, without any deduction. Let no one intercept them or delay them; for no one can take any share of the gratitude due for your gifts without robbing you of it.

V. Nothing is more bitter than long uncertainty; some can bear to have their hopes extinguished better than to have them deferred. Yet many men are led by an unworthy vanity into this fault of putting off the accomplishment of their promises, merely in order to swell the crowd of their suitors, like the ministers of royalty, who delight in prolonging the display of their own arrogance, hardly thinking themselves possessed of power unless they let each man see for a long time how powerful they are. They do nothing promptly, or at one sitting; they are indeed swift to do mischief, but slow to do good. Be sure that the comic poet speaks the most absolute truth in the verses:—

"Know you not this? If you your gifts delay,
You take thereby my gratitude away."

And the following lines, the expression of virtuous pain—a high-spirited man's misery,—

"What thou doest, do quickly;"

and:—
"Nothing in the world
Is worth this trouble; I had rather you
Refused it to me now."

When the mind begins through weariness to hate the promised benefit, or while it is wavering in expectation of it, how can it feel grateful for it? As the most refined cruelty is that which prolongs the torture, while to kill the victim at once is a kind of mercy, since the extremity of torture brings its own end with it—the interval is the worst part of the execution—so the shorter time a benefit hangs in the balance, the more grateful it is to the receiver. It is possible to look forward with anxious disquietude even to good things, and, seeing that most benefits consist in a release from some form of misery, a man destroys the value of the benefit which he confers, if he has the power to relieve us, and yet allows us to suffer or to lack pleasure longer than we need. Kindness always eager to do good, and one who acts by love naturally acts at once; he who does us good, but does it tardily and with long delays, does not do so from the heart. Thus he loses two most important things: time, and the proof of his good will to us; for a lingering consent is but a form of denial.

VI. The manner in which things are said or done, my Liberalis, forms a very important part of every transaction. We gain much by quickness, and lose much by slowness. Just as in darts, the strength of the iron head remains the same, but there is an immeasureable difference between the blow of one hurled with the full swing of the arm and one which merely drops from the hand, and the same sword either grazes or pierces according as the blow is delivered; so, in like manner, that which is given is the same, but the manner in which it is given makes the difference. How sweet, how precious is a gift, when he who gives does not permit himself to be thanked, and when while he gives he forgets that he has given! To reproach a man at the very moment that you are doing him a service is sheer madness; it is to mix insult with your favours. We ought not to make our benefits burdensome, or to add any bitterness to them. Even if there be some subject upon which you wish to warn your friend, choose some other time for doing so.

VII. Fabius Verrucosus used to compare a benefit bestowed by a harsh man in an offensive manner to a gritty loaf of bread, which a hungry man is obliged to receive, but which is painful to eat. When Marius Nepos of the praetorian guard asked Tiberius Caesar for help to pay his debts, Tiberius asked him for a list of his creditors; this is calling a meeting of creditors, not paying debts. When the list was made out, Tiberius wrote to Nepos telling him that he had ordered the money to be paid, and adding some offensive reproaches. The result of this was that Nepos owed no debts, yet received no kindness; Tiberius, indeed, relieved him from his creditors, but laid him under no obligation. Tiberius, however, had some design in doing so; I imagine he did not wish more of his friends to come to him with the same request. His mode of proceeding was, perhaps, successful in restraining men's extravagant desires by shame, but he who wishes to confer benefits must follow quite a different path. In all ways you should make your benefit as acceptable as possible by presenting it in the most attractive form; but the method of Tiberius is not to confer benefits, but to reproach.

VIII. Moreover, if incidentally I should say what I think of this part of the subject, I do not consider that it is becoming even to an emperor to give merely in order to cover a man with shame. "And yet," we are told, "Tiberius did not even by this means attain his object; for after this a good many persons were found to make the same request. He ordered all of them to explain the reasons of their indebtedness before the senate, and when they did so, granted them certain definite sums of money." This is not an act of generosity, but a reprimand. You may call it a subsidy, or an imperial contribution; it is not a benefit, for the receiver cannot think of it without shame. I was summoned before a judge, and had to be tried at bar before I obtained what I asked for.

IX. Accordingly, all writers on ethical philosophy tell us that some benefits ought to be given in secret, others in public. Those things which it is glorious to receive, such as military decorations or public offices, and whatever else gains in value the more widely it is known, should be conferred in public; on the other hand, when they do not promote a man or add to his social standing, but help him when in weakness, in want, or in disgrace, they should be given silently, and so as to be known only to those who profit by them.

X. Sometimes even the person who is assisted must be

deceived, in order that he may receive our bounty without knowing the source from whence it flows. It is said that Arcesilaus had a friend who was poor, but concealed his poverty; who was ill, yet tried to hide his disorder, and who had not money for the necessary expenses of existence. Without his knowledge, Arcesilaus placed a bag of money under his pillow, in order that this victim of false shame might rather seem to find what he wanted than to receive. "What," say you, "ought he not to know from whom he received it?" Yes; let him not know it at first, if it be essential to your kindness that he should not; afterwards I will do so much for him, and give him so much that he will perceive who was the giver of the former benefit; or, better still, let him not know that he has received any thing, provided I know that I have given it. "This," you say, "is to get too little return for one's goodness." True, if it be an investment of which you are thinking; but if a gift, it should be given in the way which will be of most service to the receiver. You should be satisfied with the approval of your own conscience; if not, you do not really delight in doing good, but in being seen to do good. "For all that," say you, "I wish him to know it." Is it a debtor that you seek for? "For all that, I wish him to know it." What! though it be more useful, more creditable, more pleasant for him not to know his benefactor, will you not consent to stand aside? "I wish him to know." So, then, you would not save a man's life in the dark? I do not deny that, whenever the matter admits of it, one ought to take into consideration the pleasure which we receive from the joy of the receiver of our kindness; but if he ought to have help and is ashamed to receive it—if what we bestow upon him pains him unless it be concealed—I forbear to make my benefits public. Why should I not refrain from hinting at my having given him anything, when the first and most essential rule is, never to reproach a man with what you have done for him, and not even to remind him of it. The rule for the giver and receiver of a benefit is, that the one should straightway forget that he has given, the other should never forget that he has received it.

XI. A constant reference to one's own services wounds our friend's feelings. Like the man who was saved from the proscription under the triumvirate by one of Caesar's friends, and afterwards found it impossible to endure his preserver's arrogance, they wish to cry, "Give me back to Caesar." How long will you go on saying, "I saved you, I snatched you from the jaws of death?" This is indeed life, if I remember it by my own will, but death if I remember it at yours; I owe you nothing, if you saved me merely in order to have some one to point at. How long do you mean to lead me about? how long do you mean to forbid me to forget my adventure? If I had been a defeated enemy, I should have been led in triumph but once. We ought not to speak of the benefits which we have conferred; to remind men of them is to ask them to return them. We should not obtrude them, or recall the memory of them; you should only remind a man of what you have given him by giving him something else. We ought not even to tell others of our good deeds. He who confers a benefit should be silent, it should be told by the receiver; for otherwise you may receive the retort which was made to one who was everywhere boasting of the benefit which he had conferred: "You will not deny," said his victim, "that you have received a return for it?" "When?" asked he. "Often," said the other, "and in many places, that is, wherever and whenever you have told the story." What need is there for you to speak, and to take the place which belongs to another? There is a man who can tell the story in a way much more to your credit, and thus you will gain glory for not telling it your self. You would think me ungrateful if, through your own silence, no one is to know of your benefit. So far from doing this, even if any one tells the story in our presence, we ought to make answer, "He does indeed deserve much more than this, and I am aware that I have not hitherto done any great things for him, although I wish to do so." This should not be said jokingly, nor yet with that air by which some persons repel those whom they especially wish to attract. In addition to this, we ought to act with the greatest politeness towards such persons. If the farmer ceases his labours after he has put in the seed, he will lose what he has sown; it is only by great pains that seeds are brought to yield a crop; no plant will bear fruit unless it be tended with equal care from first to last, and the same rule is true of benefits. Can any benefits be greater than those which children receive from their parents? Yet these benefits are useless if they be deserted while young, if the pious care of the parents does not for a long time watch over the gift which they have bestowed. So it is with other benefits; unless you help them, you will lose them; to give is not enough, you must foster what you have given. If you wish those whom you lay under an obligation to be grateful to you, you must not merely confer benefits upon them, but you must also love them. Above all, as I said before, spare their ears; you will weary them if you remind them of your goodness, if you reproach them with it you will make them hate you. Pride ought above all things to be avoided when you confer a benefit. What need have you for disdainful airs, or swelling phrases? the act itself will exalt you. Let us shun vain boasting: let us be silent, and let our deeds speak for us. A benefit conferred with haughtiness not only wins no gratitude, but causes dislike.

XII. Gaius Caesar granted Pompeius Pennus his life, that is, if not to take away life be to grant it; then, when Pompeius was set free and returning thanks to him, he stretched out his left foot to be kissed. Those who excuse this action, and say that it was not done through arrogance, say that he wished to show him a gilded, nay a golden slipper studded with pearls. "Well," say they, "what disgrace can there be in a man of consular rank kissing gold and pearls, and what part of Caesar's whole body was it less pollution to kiss?" So, then, that man, the object of whose life was to change a free state into a Persian despotism, was not satisfied when a senator, an aged man, a man who had filled the highest offices in the state, prostrated himself before him in the presence of all the nobles, just as the vanquished prostrate themselves before their conqueror! He discovered a place below his knees down to which he might thrust liberty. What is this but trampling upon the commonwealth, and that, too, with the left foot, though you may say that this point does not signify? It was not a sufficiently foul and frantic outrage for the emperor to sit at the trial of a consular for his life wearing slippers, he must needs push his shoes into a senator's face.

XIII. O pride, the silliest fault of great good fortune! how pleasant it is to take nothing from thee! how dost thou turn all benefits into outrages! how dost thou delight in all excess! how ill all things become thee! The higher thou risest the lower thou art, and provest that the good things by which thou art so puffed up profit thee not; thou spoilest all that thou givest. It is worth while to inquire why it is that pride thus swaggers and changes the form and appearance of her countenance, so that she prefers a mask to her own face. It is pleasant to receive gifts when they are conferred in a kindly and gentle manner, when a superior in giving them does not exalt himself over me, but shows as much good feeling as possible, placing himself on a level with me, giving without parade, and choosing a time when I am glad of his help, rather than waiting till I am in the bitterest need. The only way by which you can prevail upon proud men not to spoil their gifts by their arrogance is by proving to them that benefits do not appear greater because they are bestowed with great pomp and circumstance; that no one will think them greater men for so doing, and that excessive pride is a mere delusion which leads men to hate even what they ought to love.

XIV. There are some things which injure those who receive them, things which it is not a benefit to give but to withhold; we should therefore consider the usefulness of our gift rather than the wish of the petitioner to receive it; for we often long for hurtful things, and are unable to discern how ruinous they are, because our judgment is biassed by our feelings; when, however, the longing is past, when that frenzied impulse which masters our good sense has passed away, we abhor those who have given us hurtful gifts. As we refuse cold water to the sick, or swords to the grief-stricken or remorseful, and take from the insane whatever they might in their delirium use to their own destruction, so must we persist in refusing to give anything whatever that is hurtful, although our friends earnestly and humbly, nay, sometimes even most piteously beg for it. We ought to look at the end of our benefits as well as the beginning, and not merely to give what men are glad to receive, but what they will hereafter be glad to have received. There are many who say, "I know that this will do him no good, but what am I to do? he begs for it, I cannot withstand his entreaties. Let him see to it; he will blame himself, not me." Not so: you he will blame, and deservedly; when he comes to his right mind, when the frenzy which now excites him has left him, how can he help hating the man who has assisted him to harm and to endanger himself? It is a cruel kindness to allow one's self to be won over into granting that which injures those who beg for it. Just as it is the noblest of acts to save men from harm against their will, so it is but hatred, under the mask of civility, to grant what is harmful to those who ask for it. Let us confer benefits of such a kind, that the more they are made use of the better they please, and which never can turn into injuries.

I never will give money to a man if I know that he will pay it to an adulteress, nor will I be found in connexion with any wicked act or plan; if possible, I will restrain men from crime; if not, at least I will never assist them in it. Whether my friend be driven into doing wrong by anger, or seduced from the path of safety by the heat of ambition, he shall never gain the means of doing mischief except from himself, nor will I enable him one day to say, "He ruined me out of love for me." Our friends often give us what our enemies wish us to receive; we are driven by the unseasonable fondness of the former into the ruin which the latter hope will befall us. Yet, often as it is the case, what can be more shameful than that there should be no difference between a benefit and hatred?

XV. Let us never bestow gifts which may recoil upon us to our shame. As the sum total of friendship consists in making our friends equal to ourselves, we ought to consider the interests of both parties; I must give to him that wants, yet so that I do not want myself; I must help him who is perishing, yet so that I do not perish myself, unless by so doing I can save a great man or a great cause. I must give no benefit which it would disgrace me to ask for. I ought not to make a small benefit appear a great one, nor allow great benefits to be regarded as small; for although it destroys all feeling of gratitude to treat what you give like a creditor, yet you do not reproach a man, but merely set off your gift to the best advantage by letting him know what it is worth. Every man must consider what his resources and powers are, so that we may not give either more or less than we are able. We must also consider the character and position of the person to whom we give, for some men are too great to give small gifts, while others are too small to receive great ones. Compare, therefore, the character both of the giver and the receiver, and weigh that which you give between the two, taking care that what is given be neither too burdensome nor too trivial for the one to give, nor yet such as the receiver will either treat with disdain as too small, or think too great for him to deal with.

XVI. Alexander, who was of unsound mind, and always full of magnificent ideas, presented somebody with a city. When the man to whom he gave it had reflected upon the scope of his own powers, he wished to avoid the jealousy which so great a present would excite, saying that the gift did not suit a man of his position. "I do not ask," replied Alexander, "what is becoming for you to receive, but what is becoming for me to give." This seems a spirited and kingly speech, yet really it is a most foolish one. Nothing is by itself a becoming gift for any one: all depends upon who gives it, to whom he gives it, when, for what reason, where, and so forth, without which details it is impossible to argue about it. Inflated creature! if it did not become him to receive this gift, it could not become thee to give it. There should be a proportion between men's characters and the offices which they fill; and as virtue in all cases should be our measure, he who gives too much acts as wrongly as he who gives too little. Even granting that fortune has raised you so high, that, where other men give cups, you give cities (which it would show a greater mind in you not to take than to take and squander), still there must be some of your friends who are not strong enough to put a city in their pockets.

XVII. A certain cynic asked Antigonus for a talent. Antigonus answered that this was too much for a cynic to ask for. After this rebuff he asked for a penny. Antigonus answered that this was too little for a king to give. "This kind of hair-splitting" (you say) "is contemptible: he found the means of giving neither. In the matter of the penny he thought of the king, in that of the talent he thought of the cynic, whereas with respect to the cynic it would have been right to receive the penny, with respect to the king it would have been right to give the talent. Though there may be things which are too great for a cynic to receive, yet nothing is so small, that it does not become a gracious king to bestow it." If you ask me, I applaud Antigonus; for it is not to be endured that a man who despises money should ask for it. Your cynic has publicly proclaimed his hatred of money, and assumed the character of one who despises it: let him act up to his professions. It is most inconsistent for him to earn money by glorifying his poverty. I wish to use Chrysippus's simile of the game of ball, in which the ball must certainly fall by the fault either of the thrower or of the catcher; it only holds its course when it passes between the hands of two persons who each throw it and catch it suitably. It is necessary, however, for a good player to send the ball in one way to a comrade at a long distance, and in another to one at a short distance. So it is with a benefit: unless it be suitable both for the giver and the receiver, it will neither leave the one nor reach the other as it ought. If we have to do with a practised and skilled player, we shall throw the ball more recklessly, for however it may come, that quick and agile hand will send it back again; if we are playing with an unskilled novice, we shall not throw it so hard, but far more gently, guiding it straight into his very hands, and we shall run to meet it when it returns to us. This is just what we ought to do in conferring benefits; let us teach some men how to do so, and be satisfied if they attempt it, if they have the courage and the will to do so. For the most part, however, we make men ungrateful, and encourage them, to be so, as if our benefits were only great when we cannot receive any gratitude for them; just as some spiteful ball-players purposely put out their companion, of course to the ruin of the game, which cannot be carried on without entire agreement Many men are of so depraved a nature that they had rather lose the presents which they make than be thought to have received a return for them, because they are proud, and like to lay people under obligations: yet how much better and more kindly would it be if they tried to enable the others also to perform their parts, if they encouraged them in returning gratitude, put the best construction upon all their acts, received one who wished to thank them just as cordially as if he came to repay what he had received, and easily lent themselves to the belief that those whom they have laid under an obligation wish to repay it. We blame usurers equally when they press harshly for payment, and when they delay and make difficulties about taking back the money which they have lent; in the same way, it is just as right that a benefit should be returned, as it is wrong to ask any one to return it. The best man is he who gives readily, never asks for any return, and is delighted when the return is made, because, having really and truly forgotten what he gave, he receives it as though it were a present.

XVIII. Some men not only give, but even receive benefit haughtily, a mistake into which we ought not to fall: for now let us cross over to the other side of the subject, and consider how men should behave when they receive benefits. Every function which is performed by two persons makes equal demands upon both: after you have considered what a father ought to be, you will perceive that there remains an equal task, that of considering what a son ought to be: a husband has certain duties, but those of a wife are no less important. Each of these give and take equally, and each require a similar rule of life, which, as Hecaton observes, is hard to follow: indeed, it is difficult for us to attain to virtue, or even to anything that comes near virtue: for we ought not only to act virtuously but to do so upon principle. We ought to follow this guide throughout our lives, and to do everything great and small according to its dictates: according as virtue prompts us we ought both to give and to receive. Now she will declare at the outset that we ought not to receive benefits from every man. "From whom, then, ought we to receive them?" To answer you briefly, I should say, from those to whom we have given them. Let us consider whether we ought not to be even more careful in choosing to whom we should owe than to whom we should give. For even supposing that no unpleasantness should result (and very much always does), still it is a great misery to be indebted to a man to whom you do not wish to be under an obligation; whereas it is most delightful to receive a benefit from one whom you can love even after he has wronged you, and when the pleasure which you feel in his friendship is justified by the grounds on which it is based. Nothing is more wretched for a modest and honourable man than to feel it to be his duty to love one whom it does not please him to love. I must constantly remind you that I do not speak of wise men, who take pleasure in everything that is their duty, who have their feelings under command, and are able to lay down whatever law they please to themselves and keep it, but that I speak of imperfect beings struggling to follow the right path, who often have trouble in bending their passions to their will. I must therefore choose the man from whom I will accept a benefit; indeed, I ought to be more careful in the choice of my creditor for a benefit than for money; for I have only to pay the latter as much as I received of him, land when I have paid it I am free from all obligation; but to the other I must both repay more, and even when I have repaid his kindness we remain connected, for when I have paid my debt I ought again to renew it, while our friendship endures unbroken. Thus, as I ought not to make an unworthy man my friend, so I ought not to admit an unworthy man into that most holy bond of gratitude for benefits, from which friendship arises. You reply, "I cannot always say 'No': sometimes I must receive a benefit even against my will. Suppose I were given something by a cruel and easily offended tyrant, who would take it as an affront if his bounty were slighted? am I not to accept it? Suppose it were offered by a pirate, or a brigand, or a king of the temper of a pirate or brigand. What ought I to do? Such a man is not a worthy object for me to owe a benefit to." When I say that you ought to choose, I except vis major and fear, which destroy all power of choice. If you are free, if it lies with you to decide whether you will or not, then you will turn over in your own mind whether you will take a gift from a man or not; but if your position makes it impossible for you to choose, then be assured that you do not receive a gift, you merely obey orders. No one incurs any obligation by receiving what it was not in his power to refuse; if you want to know whether I wish to take it, arrange matters so that I have the power of saying 'No.' "Yet suppose he gave you your life." It does not matter what the gift was, unless it be given and received with good will: you are not my preserver because you have saved my life. Poison sometimes acts as a medicine, yet it is not on that account regarded as wholesome. Some things benefit us but put us under no obligation: for instance a man who intended to kill a tyrant, cut with his sword a tumour from which he suffered: yet the tyrant did not show him gratitude because by wounding him he had healed a disease which surgeons had feared to meddle with.

XIX. You see that the actual thing itself is not of much importance, because it is not regarded as a benefit at all, if you do good when you intended to do evil; in such a case the benefit is done by chance, the man did harm. I have seen a lion in the amphitheatre, who recognized one of the men who fought with wild beasts, who once had been his keeper, and protected him against the attacks of the other animals. Are we, then, to say that this assistance of the brute was a benefit? By no means, because it did not intend to do it, and did not do it with kindly intentions. You may class the lion and your tyrant together: each of them saved a man's life, yet neither conferred a benefit. Because it is not a benefit to be forced to receive one, neither is it a benefit to be under an obligation to a man to whom we do not wish to be indebted. You must first give me personal freedom of decision, and then your benefit.

XX. The question has been raised, whether Marcus Brutus ought to have received his life from the hands of Julius Caesar, who, he had decided, ought to be put to death.

As to the grounds upon which he put him to death, I shall discuss them elsewhere; for to my mind, though he was in other respects a great man, in this he seems to have been entirely wrong, and not to have followed the maxims of the Stoic philosophy. He must either have feared the name of "King," although a state thrives best under a good king, or he must have hoped that liberty could exist in a state where some had so much to gain by reigning, and others had so much to gain by becoming slaves. Or, again, he must have supposed that it would be possible to restore the ancient constitution after all the ancient manners had been lost, and that citizens could continue to possess equal rights, or laws remain inviolate, in a state in which he had seen so many thousands of men fighting to decide, not whether they should be slaves or free, but which master they should serve. How forgetful he seems to have been, both of human nature and of the history of his own country, in supposing that when one despot was destroyed another of the same temper would not take his place, though, after so many kings had perished by lightning and the sword, a Tarquin was found to reign! Yet Brutus did right in receiving his life from Caesar, though he was not bound thereby to regard Caesar as his father, since it was by a wrong that Caesar had come to be in a position to bestow this benefit. A man does not save your life who does not kill you; nor does he confer a benefit, but merely gives you your discharge. [The 'discharge' alluded to is that which was granted to the beaten one of a pair of gladiators, when their duel was not to the death.]

XXI. It seems to offer more opportunity for debate to consider what a captive ought to do, if a man of abominable vices offers him the price of his ransom? Shall I permit myself to be saved by a wretch? When safe, what recompense can I make to him? Am I to live with an infamous person? Yet, am I not to live with my preserver? I will tell you my opinion. I would accept money, even from such a person, if it were to save my life; yet I would only accept it as a loan, not as a benefit. I would repay him the money, and if I were ever able to preserve him from danger I would do so. As for friendship, which can only exist between equals, I would not condescend to be such a man's friend; nor would I regard him as my preserver, but merely as a money-lender, to whom I am only bound to repay what I borrowed from him.

A man may be a worthy person for me to receive a benefit from, but it will hurt him to give it. For this reason I will not receive it, because he is ready to help me to his own prejudice, or even danger. Suppose that he is willing to plead for me in court, but by so doing will make the king his enemy. I should be his enemy, if, when he is willing to risk himself for me, if I were not to risk myself without him, which moreover is easier for me to do.

As an instance of this, Hecaton calls the case of Arcesilaus silly, and not to the purpose. Arcesilaus, he says, refused to receive a large sum of money which was offered to him by a son, lest the son should offend his penurious father. What did he do deserving of praise, in not receiving stolen goods, in choosing not to receive them, instead of returning them? What proof of self-restraint is there in refusing to receive another man's property. If you want an instance of magnanimity, take the case of Julius Graecinus, whom Caius Caesar put to death merely on the ground that he was a better man than it suited a tyrant for anyone to be. This man, when he was receiving subscriptions from many of his friends to cover his expenses in exhibiting public games, would not receive a large sum which was sent him by Fabius Persicus; and when he was blamed for rejecting it by those who think more of what is given than of who gives it, he answered, "Am I to accept a present from a man when I would not accept his offer to drink a glass of wine with him?"

When a consular named Rebilius, a man of equally bad character, sent a yet larger sum to Graecinus, and pressed him to receive it. "I must beg," answered he, "that you will excuse me. I did not take money from Persicus either." Ought we to call this receiving presents, or rather taking one's pick of the senate?

XXII. When we have decided to accept, let us accept with cheerfulness, showing pleasure, and letting the giver see it, so that he may at once receive some return for his goodness: for as it is a good reason for rejoicing to see our friend happy, it is a better one to have made him so. Let us, therefore, show how acceptable a gift is by loudly expressing our gratitude for it; and let us do so, not only in the hearing of the giver, but everywhere. He who receives a benefit with gratitude, repays the first instalment of it.

XXIII. There are some, who only like to receive benefits privately: they dislike having any witnesses and confidants. Such men, we may believe, have no good intentions. As a giver is justified in dwelling upon those qualities of his gift which will please the receiver, so a man, when he receives, should do so publicly; you should not take from a man what you are ashamed to owe him. Some return thanks to one stealthily, in a corner, in a whisper. This is not modesty, but a kind of denying of the debt: it is the part of an ungrateful man not to express his gratitude before witnesses. Some object to any accounts being kept between them and their benefactors, and wish no brokers to be employed or witnesses to be called, but merely to give their own signature to a receipt. Those men do the like, who take care to let as few persons as possible know of the benefits which they have received. They fear to receive them in public, in order that their success may be attributed rather to their own talents than to the help of others: they are very seldom to be found in attendance upon those to whom they owe their lives and their fortunes, and thus, while avoiding the imputation of servility, they incur that of ingratitude.

XXIV. Some men speak in the most offensive terms of those to whom they owe most. There are men whom it is safer to affront than to serve, for their dislike leads them to assume the airs of persons who are not indebted to us: although nothing more is expected of them than that they should remember what they owe us, refreshing their memory from time to time, because no one can be grateful who forgets a kindness, and he who remembers it, by so doing proves his gratitude. We ought neither to receive benefits with a fastidious air, nor yet with a slavish humility: for if a man does not care for a benefit when it is freshly bestowed—a time at which all presents please us most—what will he do when its first charms have gone off? Others receive with an air of disdain, as much as to say. "I do not want it; but as you wish it so very much, I will allow you to give it to me." Others take benefits languidly, and leave the giver in doubt as to whether they know that they have received them; others barely open their lips in thanks, and would be less offensive if they said nothing. One ought to proportion one's thanks to the importance of the benefit received, and to use the phrases, "You have laid more of us than you think under an obligation," for everyone likes to find his good actions extend further than he expected. "You do not know what it is that you have done for me; but you ought to know how much more important it is than you imagine." It is in itself an expression of gratitude to speak of one's self as overwhelmed by kindness; or "I shall never be able to thank you sufficiently; but, at any rate, I will never cease to express everywhere my inability to thank you."

XXV. By nothing did Furnius gain greater credit with Augustus, and make it easy for him to obtain anything else for which he might ask, than by merely saying, when at his request Augustus pardoned his father for having taken Antonius's side, "One wrong alone I have received at your hands, Caesar; you have forced me to live and to die owing you a greater debt of gratitude than I can ever repay." What can prove gratitude so well as that a man should never be satisfied, should never even entertain the hope of making any adequate return for what he has received? By these and similar expressions we must try not to conceal our gratitude, but to display it as clearly as possible. No words need be used; if we only feel as we ought, our thankfulness will be shown in our countenances. He who intends to be grateful, let him think how he shall repay a kindness while he is receiving it. Chrysippus says that such a man must watch for his opportunity, and spring forward whenever it offers, like one who has been entered for a race, and who stands at the starting-point waiting for the barriers to be thrown open; and even then he must use great exertions and great swiftness to catch the other, who has a start of him.

XXVI. We must now consider what is the main cause of ingratitude. It is caused by excessive self-esteem, by that fault innate in all mortals, of taking a partial view of ourselves and our own acts, by greed, or by jealousy.

Let us begin with the first of these. Every one is prejudiced in his own favour, from which it follows that he believes himself to have earned all that he receives, regards it as payment for his services, and does not think that he has been appraised at a valuation sufficiently near his own. "He has given me this," says he, "but how late, after how much toil? how much more might I have earned if I had attached myself to So and so, or to So and so? I did not expect this; I have been treated like one of the herd; did he really think that I only deserved so little? why, it would have been less insulting to have passed me over altogether."

XXVII. The augur Cnaeus Lentulus, who, before his freedmen

reduced him to poverty, was one of the richest of men, who saw himself in possession of a fortune of four hundred millions—I say advisedly, "saw," for he never did more than see it—was as barren and contemptible in intellect as he was in spirit. Though very avaricious, yet he was so poor a speaker that he found it easier to give men coins than words. This man, who owed all his prosperity to the late Emperor Augustus, to whom he had brought only poverty, encumbered with a noble name, when he had risen to be the chief man in Rome, both in wealth and influence, used sometimes to complain that Augustus had interrupted his legal studies, observing that he had not received anything like what he had lost by giving up the study of eloquence. Yet the truth was that Augustus, besides loading him with other gifts, had set him free from the necessity of making himself ridiculous by labouring at a profession in which he never could succeed.

Greed does not permit any one to be grateful; for what is given is never equal to its base desires, and the more we receive the more we covet, for avarice is much more eager when it has to deal with great accumulations of wealth, just as the power of a flame is enormously greater in proportion to the size of the conflagration from which it springs. Ambition in like manner suffers no man to rest satisfied with that measure of public honours, to gain which was once the limit of his wildest hope; no one is thankful for becoming tribune, but grumbles at not being at once promoted to the post of praetor; nor is he grateful for this if the consulship does not follow; and even this does not satisfy him if he be consul but once. His greed ever stretches itself out further, and he does not understand the greatness of his success because he always looks forward to the point at which he aims, and never back towards that from which he started.

XXVIII. A more violent and distressing vice than any of these is jealousy which disturbs us by suggesting comparisons. "He gave me this, but he gave more to that man, and he gave it to him before me;" after which he sympathises with no one, but pushes his own claims to the prejudice of every one else. How much more straightforward and modest is it to make the most of what we have received, knowing that no man is valued so highly by any one else as by his own self! "I ought to have received more, but it was not easy for him to give more; he was obliged to distribute his liberality among many persons. This is only the beginning; let me be contented, and by my gratitude encourage him to show me more favour; he has not done as much as he ought, but he will do so the more frequently; he certainly preferred that man to me, but he has preferred me before many others; that man is not my equal either in virtue or in services, but he has some charm of his own: by complaining I shall not make myself deserve to receive more, but shall become unworthy of what I have received. More has been given to those most villainous men than has been given to me; well, what is that to the purpose? how seldom does Fortune show judgment in her choice? We complain every day of the success of bad men; very often the hail passes over the estates of the greatest villains and strikes down the crops of the best of men; every man has to take his chance, in friendship as well as in everything else." There is no benefit so great that spitefulness can pick no holes in it, none so paltry that it cannot be made more of by friendly interpretation. We shall never want a subject for complaint if we look at benefits on their wrong side.

XXIX. See how unjustly the gifts of heaven are valued even by some who profess themselves philosophers, who complain that we are not as big as elephants, as swift as stags, as light as birds, as strong as bulls; that the skins of seals are stronger, of hinds prettier, of bears thicker, of beavers softer than ours; that dogs excel us in delicacy of scent, eagles in keenness of sight, crows in length of days, and many beasts in ease of swimming. And although nature itself does not allow some qualities, as for example strength and swiftness, to be combined in the same person, yet they call it a monstrous thing that men are not compounded of different and inconsistent good qualities, and call the gods neglectful of us because we have not been given health which even our vices cannot destroy, or knowledge of the future. They scarcely refrain from rising to such a pitch of impudence as to hate nature because we are below the gods, and not on an equality with them. How much better is it to turn to the contemplation of so many great blessings, and to be thankful that the gods have been pleased to give us a place second only to themselves in this most beautiful abode, and that they have appointed us to be the lords of the earth! Can any one compare us with the animals over whom we rule? Nothing has been denied us except what could not have been granted. In like manner, thou that takest an unfair view of the lot of mankind, think what blessings our Father has bestowed upon us, how far more powerful animals than ourselves we have broken to harness, how we catch those which are far swifter, how nothing that has life is placed beyond the reach of our weapons! We have received so many excellencies, so many crafts, above all our mind, which can pierce at once whatever it is directed against, which is swifter than the stars in their courses, for it arrives before them at the place which they will reach after many ages; and besides this, so many fruits of the earth, so much treasure, such masses of various things piled one upon another. You may go through the whole order of nature, and since you find no entire creature which you would prefer to be, you may choose from each, the special qualities which you would like to be given to yourself; then, if you rightly appreciate the partiality of nature for you, you cannot but confess yourself to be her spoiled child. So it is; the immortal gods have unto this day always held us most dear, and have bestowed upon us the greatest possible honour, a place nearest to themselves. We have indeed received great things, yet not too great.

XXX. I have thought it necessary, my friend Liberalis, to state these facts, both because when speaking of small benefits one ought to make some mention of the greatest, and because also this shameless and hateful vice (of ingratitude), starting with these, transfers itself from them to all the rest. If a man scorn these, the greatest of all benefits, to whom will he feel gratitude, what gift will he regard as valuable or deserving to be returned: to whom will he be grateful for his safety or his life, if he denies that he has received from the gods that existence which he begs from them daily? He, therefore, who teaches men to be grateful, pleads the cause not only of men, but even of the gods, for though they, being placed above all desires, cannot be in want of anything, yet we can nevertheless offer them our gratitude.

No one is justified in seeking an excuse for ingratitude in his own weakness or poverty, or in saying, "What am I to do, and how? When can I repay my debt to my superiors the lords of heaven and earth?" Avaricious as you are, it is easy for you to give them thanks, without expense; lazy though you be, you can do it without labour. At the same instant at which you received your debt towards them, if you wish to repay it, you have done as much as any one can do, for he returns a benefit who receives it with good will.

XXXI. This paradox of the Stoic philosophy, that he returns a benefit who receives it with good will, is, in my opinion, either far from admirable, or else it is incredible. For if we look at everything merely from the point of view of our intentions, every man has done as much as he chose to do; and since filial piety, good faith, justice, and in short every virtue is complete within itself, a man may be grateful in intention even though he may not be able to lift a hand to prove his gratitude. Whenever a man obtains what he aimed at, he receives the fruit of his labour. When a man bestows a benefit, at what does he aim? clearly to be of service and afford pleasure to him upon whom he bestows it. If he does what he wishes, if his purpose reaches me and fills us each with joy, he has gained his object. He does not wish anything to be given to him in return, or else it becomes an exchange of commodities, not a bestowal of benefits. A man steers well who reaches the port for which he started: a dart hurled by a steady hand performs its duty if it hits the mark; one who bestows a benefit wishes it to be received with gratitude; he gets what he wanted if it be well received. "But," you say, "he hoped for some profit also." Then it was not a benefit, the property of which is to think nothing of any repayment. I receive what was given me in the same spirit in which it was given: then I have repaid it. If this be not true, then this best of deeds has this worst of conditions attached to it, that it depends entirely upon fortune whether I am grateful or not, for if my fortune is adverse I can make no repayment. The intention is enough. What then? am I not to do whatever I may be able to repay it, and ought I not ever to be on the watch for an opportunity of filling the bosom [Footnote: Sinus, the fold of the toga over the breast, used as a pocket by the Romans. The great French actor Talma, when dressed for the first time in correct classical costume, indignantly asked where he was to put his snuff-box.] of him from whom I have received any kindness? True; but a benefit is in an evil plight if we cannot be grateful for it even when we are empty-handed.

XXXII. "A man," it is argued, "who has received a benefit, however gratefully he may have received it, has not yet accomplished all his duty, for there remains the part of repayment; just as in playing at ball it is something to catch the ball cleverly and carefully, but a man is not called a good player unless he can handily and quickly send back the ball which he has caught." This analogy is imperfect; and why? Because to do this creditably depends upon the movement and activity of the body, and not upon the mind: and an act of which we judge entirely by the eye, ought to be all clearly displayed. But if a man caught the ball as he ought to do, I should not call him a bad player for not returning it, if his delay in returning it was not caused by his own fault. "Yet," say you, "although the player is not wanting in skill, because he did one part of his duty, and was able to do the other part, yet in such a case the game is imperfect, for its perfection lies in sending the ball backwards and forwards." I am unwilling to expose this fallacy further; let us think that it is the game, not the player that is imperfect: so likewise in the subject which we are discussing, the thing which is given lacks something, because another equal thing ought to be returned for it, but the mind of the giver lacks nothing, because it has found another mind equal to itself, and as far as intentions go, has effected what it wished.

XXXIII. A man bestows a benefit upon me: I receive it just as he wished it to be received: then he gets at once what he wanted, and the only thing which he wanted, and therefore I have proved myself grateful. After this it remains for me to enjoy my own resources, with the addition of an advantage conferred upon me by one whom I have obliged; this advantage is not the remainder of an imperfect service, but an addition to a perfected service. [Footnote: Nothing is wanted to make a benefit, conferred from good motives, perfect: if it is returned, the gratitude is to be counted as net profit.] For example, Phidias makes a statue. Now the product of an art is one thing, and that of a trade is another. It is the business of the art to make the thing which he wished to make, and that of the trade to make it with a profit. Phidias has completed his work, even though he does not sell it. The product, therefore, of his work is threefold: there is the consciousness of having made it, which he receives when his work is completed; there is the fame which he receives; and thirdly, the advantage which he obtains by it, in influence, or by selling it, or otherwise. In like manner the first fruit of a benefit is the consciousness of it, which we feel when we have bestowed it upon the person whom we chose; secondly and thirdly there is the credit which we gain by doing so, and there are those things which we may receive in exchange for it. So when a benefit has been graciously received, the giver has already received gratitude, but has not yet received recompense for it: that which we owe in return is therefore something apart from the benefit itself, for we have paid for the benefit itself when we accept it in a grateful spirit.

XXXIV. "What," say you, "can a man repay a benefit, though he does nothing?" He has taken the first step, he has offered you a good thing with good feeling, and, which is the characteristic of friendship, has placed you both on the same footing. In the next place, a benefit is not repaid in the same manner as a loan: you have no reason for expecting me to offer you any payment; the account between us depends upon the feelings alone. What I say will not appear difficult, although it may not at first accord with your ideas, if you will do me the favour to remember that there are more things than there are words to express them. There is an enormous mass of things without names, which we do not speak of under distinctive names of their own, but by the names of other things transferred to them. We speak of our own foot, of the foot of a couch, of a sail, or of a poem; we apply the word 'dog' to a hound, a fish, and a star. Because we have not enough words to assign a separate name to each thing, we borrow a name whenever we want one. Bravery is the virtue which rightly despises danger, or the science of repelling, sustaining, or inviting dangers: yet we call a brave man a gladiator, and we use the same word for a good-for-nothing slave, who is led by rashness to defy death. Economy is the science of avoiding unnecessary expenditure, or the art of using one's income with moderation: yet we call a man of mean and narrow mind, most economical, although there is an immeasurable distance between moderation and meanness. These things are naturally distinct, yet the poverty of our language compels us to call both these men economical, just as he who views slight accidents with rational contempt, and he who without reason runs into danger are alike called brave. Thus a benefit is both a beneficent action, and also is that which is bestowed by that action, such as money, a house, an office in the state: there is but one name for them both, though their force and power are widely different.

XXXV. Wherefore, give me your attention, and you will soon perceive that I say nothing to which you can object. That benefit which consists of the action is repaid when we receive it graciously; that other, which consists of something material, we have not then repaid, but we hope to do so. The debt of goodwill has been discharged by a return of goodwill; the material debt demands a material return. Thus, although we may declare that he who has received a benefit with good-will has returned the favour, yet we counsel him to return to the giver something of the same kind as that which he has received. Some part of what we have said departs from the conventional line of thought, and then rejoins it by another path. We declare that a wise man cannot receive an injury; yet, if a man hits him with his fist, that man will be found guilty of doing him an injury. We declare that a fool can possess nothing; yet if a man stole anything from a fool, we should find that man guilty of theft. We declare that all men are mad, yet we do not dose all men with hellebore; but we put into the hands of these very persons, whom we call madmen, both the right of voting and of pronouncing judgment. Similarly, we say that a man who has received a benefit with good-will has returned the favour, yet we leave him in debt nevertheless—bound to repay it even though he has repaid it. This is not to disown benefits, but is an encouragement to us neither to fear to receive benefits, nor to faint under the too great burden of them. "Good things have been given to me; I have been preserved from starving; I have been saved from the misery of abject poverty; my life, and what is dearer than life, my liberty, has been preserved. How shall I be able to repay these favours? When will the day come upon which I can prove my gratitude to him?" When a man speaks thus, the day has already come. Receive a benefit, embrace it, rejoice, not that you have received it, but that you have to owe it and return it; then you will never be in peril of the great sin of being rendered ungrateful by mischance. I will not enumerate any difficulties to you, lest you should despair, and faint at the prospect of a long and laborious servitude. I do not refer you to the future; do it with what means you have at hand. You never will be grateful unless you are so straightway. What, then, will you do? You need not take up arms, yet perhaps you may have to do so; you need not cross the seas, yet it may be that you will pay your debt, even when the wind threatens to blow a gale. Do you wish to return the benefit? Then receive it graciously; you have then returned the favour—not, indeed, so that you can think yourself to have repaid it, but so that you can owe it with a quieter conscience.

BOOK III.

I.

Not to return gratitude for benefits, my AEbutius Liberalis, is both base in itself, and is thought base by all men; wherefore even ungrateful men complain of ingratitude, and yet what all condemn is at the same time rooted in all; and so far do men sometimes run into the other extreme that some of them become our bitterest enemies, not merely after receiving benefits from us, but because they have received them. I cannot deny that some do this out of sheer badness of nature; but more do so because lapse of time destroys their remembrance, for time gradually effaces what they felt vividly at the moment. I remember having had an argument with you about this class of persons, whom you wished to call forgetful rather than ungrateful, as if that which caused a man to be ungrateful was any excuse for his being so, or as if the fact of this happening to a man prevented his being ungrateful, when we know that it only happens to ungrateful men. There are many classes of the ungrateful, as there are of thieves or of homicides, who all have the same fault, though there is a great variety in its various forms. The man is ungrateful who denies that he has received a benefit; who pretends that he has not received it; who does not return it. The most ungrateful man of all is he who forgets it. The others, though they do not repay it, yet feel their debt, and possess some traces of worth, though obstructed by their bad conscience. They may by some means and at some time be brought to show their gratitude, if, for instance, they be pricked by shame, if they conceive some noble ambition such as occasionally rises even in the breasts of the wicked, if some easy opportunity of doing so offers; but the man from whom all recollection of the benefit has passed away can never become grateful. Which of the two do you call the worse—he who is ungrateful for kindness, or he who does not even remember it? The eyes which fear to look at the light are diseased, but those which cannot see it are blind. It is filial impiety not to love one's parents, but not to recognise them is madness.

II. Who is so ungrateful as he who has so completely laid aside and cast away that which ought to be in the forefront of his mind and ever before him, that he knows it not? It is clear that if forgetfulness of a benefit steals over a man, he cannot have often thought about repaying it.

In short, repayment requires gratitude, time, opportunity, and the help of fortune; whereas, he who remembers a benefit is grateful for it, and that too without expenditure. Since gratitude demands neither labour, wealth, nor good fortune, he who fails to render it has no excuse behind which to shelter himself; for he who places a benefit so far away that it is out of his sight, never could have meant to be grateful for it. Just as those tools which are kept in use, and are daily touched by the hand, are never in danger of growing rusty, while those which are not brought before our eyes, and lie as if superfluous, not being required for common use, collect dirt by the mere lapse of time, so likewise that which our thoughts frequently turn over and renew never passes from our memory, which only loses those things to which it seldom directs its eyes.

III. Besides this, there are other causes which at times erase the greatest services from our minds. The first and most powerful of these is that, being always intent upon new objects of desire, we think, not of what we have, but of what we are striving to obtain. Those whose mind is fixed entirely upon what they hope to gain, regard with contempt all that is their own already. It follows that since men's eagerness for something new makes them undervalue whatever they have received, they do not esteem those from whom they have received it. As long as we are satisfied with the position we have gained, we love our benefactor, we look up to him, and declare that we owe our position entirely to him; then we begin to entertain other aspirations, and hurry forward to attain them after the manner of human beings, who when they have gained much always covet more; straightway all that we used to regard as benefits slip from our memory, and we no longer consider the advantages which we enjoy over others, but only the insolent prosperity of those who have outstripped us. Now no one can at the same time be both jealous and grateful, because those who are jealous are querulous and sad, while the grateful are joyous. In the next place, since none of us think of any time but the present, and but few turn back their thoughts to the past, it results that we forget our teachers, and all the benefits which we have obtained from them, because we have altogether left our childhood behind us: thus, all that was done for us in our youth perishes unremembered, because our youth itself is never reviewed. What has been is regarded by every one, not only as past, but as gone; and for the same reason, our memory is weak for what is about to happen in the future.

IV. Here I must do Epicurus the justice to say that he constantly complains of our ingratitude for past benefits, because we cannot bring back again, or count among our present pleasures, those good things which we have received long ago, although no pleasures can be more undeniable than those which cannot be taken from us. Present good is not yet altogether complete, some mischance may interrupt it; the future is in suspense, and uncertain; but what is past is laid up in safety. How can any man feel gratitude for benefits, if he skips through his whole life entirely engrossed with the present and the future? It is remembrance that makes men grateful; and the more men hope, the less they remember.

V. In the same way, my Liberalis, as some things remain in our memory as soon as they are learned, while to know others it is not enough to have learned them, for our knowledge slips away from us unless it be kept up—I allude to geometry and astronomy, and such other sciences as are Hard to remember because of their intricacy—so the greatness of some benefits prevents their being forgotten, while others, individually less, though many more in number, and bestowed at different times, pass from our minds, because, as I have stated above, we do not constantly think about them, and do not willingly recognize how much we owe to each of our benefactors. Listen to the words of those who ask for favours. There is not one of them who does not declare that his remembrance will be eternal, who does not vow himself your devoted servant and slave, or find, if he can, some even greater expression of humility with which to pledge himself. After a brief space of time these same men avoid their former expressions, thinking them abject, and scarcely befitting free-born men; afterwards they arrive at the same point to which, as I suppose, the worst and most ungrateful of men come—that is, they forget. So little does forgetfulness excuse ingratitude, that even the remembrance of a benefit may leave us ungrateful.

VI. The question has been raised, whether this most odious vice ought to go unpunished; and whether the law commonly made use of in the schools, by which we can proceed against a man for ingratitude, ought to be adopted by the State also, since all men agree that it is just. "Why not?" you may say, "seeing that even cities cast in each other's teeth the services which they have performed to one another, and demand from the children some return for benefits conferred upon their fathers?" On the other hand, our ancestors, who were most admirable men, made demands upon their enemies alone, and both gave and lost their benefits with magnanimity. With the exception of Macedonia, no nation has ever established an action at law for ingratitude. And this is a strong argument against its being established, because all agree in blaming crime; and homicide, poisoning, parricide, and sacrilege are visited with different penalties in different countries, but everywhere with some penalty; whereas this most common vice is nowhere punished, though it is everywhere blamed. We do not acquit it; but as it would be most difficult to reckon accurately the penalty for so varying a matter, we condemn it only to be hated, and place it upon the list of those crimes which we refer for judgment to the gods.

VII. Many arguments occur to me which prove that this vice ought not to come under the action of the law. First of all, the best part of a benefit is lost if the benefit can be sued for at law, as in the case of a loan, or of letting and hiring. Indeed, the finest part of a benefit is that we have given it without considering whether we shall lose it or not, that we have left all this to the free choice of him who receives it: if I call him before a judge, it begins to be not a benefit, but a loan. Next, though it is a most honourable thing to show gratitude, it ceases to be honourable if it be forced, for in that case no one will praise a grateful man any more than he praises him who restores the money which was deposited in his keeping, or who pays what he borrowed without the intervention of a judge. We should therefore spoil the two finest things in human life,—a grateful man and a beneficent man; for what is there admirable in one who does not give but merely lends a benefit, or in one who repays it, not because he wishes, but because he is forced to do so? There is no credit in being grateful, unless it is safe to be ungrateful. Besides this, all the courts would hardly be enough for the action of this one law. Who would not plead under it? Who would not be pleaded against? for every one exalts his own merits, every one magnifies even the smallest matters which he has bestowed upon another. Besides this, those things which form the subject of a judicial inquiry can be distinctly defined, and cannot afford unlimited licence to the judge; wherefore a good cause is in a better position if it before a judge than before an arbitrator, because the words of the law tie down a judge and define certain limits beyond which he may not pass, whereas the conscience of an arbitrator is free and not fettered by any rules, so that he can either give or take away, and can arrange his decision, not according to the precepts of law and justice, but just as his own kindly feeling or compassion may prompt him. An action for ingratitude would not bind a judge, but would place him in the position of an autocrat. It cannot be known what or how great a benefit is; all that would be really important would be, how indulgently the judge might interpret it. No law defines an ungrateful person, often, indeed, one who repays what he has received is ungrateful, and one who has not returned it is grateful. Even an unpractised judge can give his vote upon some matters; for instance, when the thing to be determined is whether something has or has not been done, when a dispute is terminated by the parties giving written bonds, or when the casting up of accounts decides between the disputants. When, however, motives have to be guessed at, when matters upon which wisdom alone can decide, are brought into court, they cannot be tried by a judge taken at random from the list of "select judges," [Footnote: See Smith's "Dict. of Antiq.," s. v] whom property and the inheritance of an equestrian fortune [Footnote: 400,000 sesterces] has placed upon the roll.

VIII. Ingratitude, therefore, is not only matter unfit to be brought into court, but no judge could be found fit to try it; and this you will not be surprised at, if you examine the difficulties of any one who should attempt to prosecute a man upon such a charge. One man may have given a large sum of money, but he is rich and would not feel it; another may have given it at the cost of his entire inheritance. The sum given is the same in each case, but the benefit conferred is not the same. Add another instance: suppose that to redeem a debtor from slavery one man paid money from his own private means, while another man paid the same sum, but had to borrow it or beg for it, and allow himself to be laid under a great obligation to some one; would you rank the man who so easily bestowed his benefit on an equality with him who was obliged to receive a benefit himself before he could bestow it? Some benefits are great, not because of their amount, but because of the time at which they are bestowed; it is a benefit to give an estate whose fertility can bring down the price of corn, and it is a benefit to give a loaf of bread in time of famine; it is a benefit to give provinces through which flow vast navigable rivers, and it is a benefit, when men are parched with thirst, and can scarcely draw breath through their dry throats, to show them a spring of water. Who will compare these cases with one another, or weigh one against the other? It is hard to give a decision when it is not the thing given, but its meaning, which has to be considered; though what is given is the same, yet if it be given under different circumstances it has a different value. A man may have bestowed a benefit upon me, but unwillingly; he may have complained of having given it; he may have looked at me with greater haughtiness than he was wont to do; he may have been so slow in giving it, that he would have done me a greater service if he had promptly refused it. How could a judge estimate the value of these things, when words, hesitation, or looks can destroy all their claim to gratitude?

IX. What, again, could he do, seeing that some things are called benefits because they are unduly coveted, whilst others are not benefits at all, according to this common valuation, yet are of even greater value, though not so showy? You call it a benefit to cause a man to be adopted as a member of a powerful city, to get him enrolled among the knights, or to defend one who is being tried for his life: what do you say of him who gives useful advice? of him who holds you back when you would rush into crime? of him who strikes the sword from the hands of the suicide? of him who by his power of consolation brings back to the duties of life one who was plunged in grief, and eager to follow those whom he had lost? of him who sits at the bedside of the sick man, and who, when health and recovery depend upon seizing the right moment, administers food in due season, stimulates the failing veins with wine, or calls in the physician to the dying man? Who can estimate the value of such services as these? who can bid us weigh dissimilar benefits one with another? "I gave you a house," says one. Yes, but I forewarned you that your own house would come down upon your head. "I gave you an estate," says he. True, but I gave a plank to you when shipwrecked. "I fought for you and received wounds for you," says another. But I saved your life by keeping silence. Since a benefit is both given and returned differently by different people, it is hard to make them balance.

X. Besides this, no day is appointed for repayment of a benefit, as there is for borrowed money; consequently he who has not yet repaid a benefit may do so hereafter: for tell me, pray, within what time a man is to be declared ungrateful? The greatest benefits cannot be proved by evidence; they often lurk in the silent consciousness of two men only; are we to introduce the rule of not bestowing benefits without witnesses? Next, what punishment are we to appoint for the ungrateful? is there to be one only for all, though the benefits which they have received are different? or should the punishment be varying, greater or less according to the benefit which each has received? Are our valuations to be restricted to pecuniary fines? what are we to do, seeing that in some cases the benefit conferred is life, and things dearer than life? What punishment is to be assigned to ingratitude for these? One less than the benefit? That would be unjust. One equal to it; death? What could be more inhuman than to cause benefits to result in cruelty?

XI. It may be argued, "Parents have certain privileges: these are regarded as exempt from the action of ordinary rules, and so also ought to be the case with other beneficent persons." Nay; mankind has assigned a peculiar sanctity to the position of parents, because it was advantageous that children should be reared, and people had to be tempted into undergoing the toil of doing so, because the issue of their experiment was doubtful. One cannot say to them, as one does to others who bestow benefits, "Choose the man to whom you give: you must only blame yourself if you are deceived; help the deserving." In rearing children nothing depends upon the judgment of those who rear them; it is a matter of hope: in order, therefore, that people may be more willing to embark upon this lottery, it was right that they should be given a certain authority; and since it is useful for youth to be governed, we have placed their parents in the position of domestic magistrates, under whose guardianship their lives may be ruled. Moreover, the position of parents differs from that of other benefactors, for their having given formerly to their children does not stand in the way of their giving now and hereafter; and also, there is no fear of their falsely asserting that they have given: with others one has to inquire not only whether they have received, but whether they have given; but the good deeds of parents are placed beyond doubt. In the next place, one benefit bestowed by parents is the same for all, and might be counted once for all; while the others which they bestow are of various kinds, unlike one to another, differing from one another by the widest possible intervals; they can therefore come under no regular rule, since it would be more just to leave them all unrewarded than to give the same reward to all.

XII. Some benefits cost much to the givers, some are of much value to the receivers but cost the givers nothing. Some are bestowed upon friends, others on strangers: now although that which is given be the same, yet it becomes more when it is given to one with whom you are beginning to be acquainted through the benefits which you have previously conferred upon him. One man may give us help, another distinctions, a third consolation. You may find one who thinks nothing pleasanter or more important than to have some one to save him from distress; you may again find one who would rather be helped to great place than to security; while some consider themselves more indebted to those who save their lives than to those who save their honour. Each of these services will be held more or less important, according as the disposition of our judge inclines to one or the other of them. Besides this, I choose my creditors for myself, whereas I often receive benefits from those from whom I would not, and sometimes I am laid under an obligation without my knowledge. What will you do in such a case? When a man has received a benefit unknown to himself, and which, had he known of it, he would have refused to receive, will you call him ungrateful if he does not repay it, however he may have received it? Suppose that some one has bestowed a benefit upon me, and that the same man has afterwards done me some wrong; am I to be bound by his one bounty to endure with patience any wrong that he may do me, or will it be the same as if I had repaid it, because he himself has by the subsequent wrong cancelled his own benefit? How, in that case, would you decide which was the greater; the present which the man has received, or the injury which has been done him? Time would fail me if I attempted to discuss all the difficulties which would arise.

XIII. It may be argued that "we render men less willing to confer benefits by not supporting the claim of those which have been bestowed to meet with gratitude, and by not punishing those who repudiate them." But you would find, on the other hand, that men would be far less willing to receive benefits, if by so doing they were likely to incur the danger of having to plead their cause in court, and having more difficulty in proving their integrity. This legislation would also render us less willing to give: for no one is willing to give to those who are unwilling to receive, but one who is urged to acts of kindness by his own good nature and by the beauty of charity, will give all the more freely to those who need make no return unless they choose. It impairs the credit of doing a service, if in doing it we are carefully protected from loss.

XIV. "Benefits, then, will be fewer, but more genuine: well, what harm is there in restricting people from giving recklessly?" Even those who would have no legislation upon the subject follow this rule, that we ought to be somewhat careful in giving, and in choosing those upon whom we bestow favours. Reflect over and over again to whom you are giving: you will have no remedy at law, no means of enforcing repayment. You are mistaken if you suppose that the judge will assist you: no law will make full restitution to you, you must look only to the honour of the receiver. Thus only can benefits retain their influence, and thus only are they admirable: you dishonour them if you make them the grounds of litigation, "Pay what you owe" is a most just proverb; and one which carries with it the sanction of all nations; but in dealing with benefits it is most shameful. "Pay!" How is a man to pay who owes his life, his position, his safety, or his reason to another? None of the greatest benefits can be repaid.

"Yet," it is said, "you ought to give in return for them something of equal value." This is just what I have been saying, that the grandeur of the act is ruined if we make our benefits commercial transactions. We ought not to encourage ourselves in avarice, in discontent, or in quarrels; the human mind is prone enough to these by nature. As far as we are able, let us check it, and cut off the opportunities for which it seeks.

XV. Would that we could indeed persuade men to receive back money which they have lent from those debtors only who are willing to pay! would that no agreement ever bound the buyer to the seller, and that their interests were not protected by sealed covenants and agreements, but rather by honour and a sense of justice! However, men prefer what is needful to what is truly best, and choose rather to force their creditors to keep faith with them than to trust that they will do so. Witnesses are called on both sides; the one, by calling in brokers, makes several names appear in his accounts as his debtors instead of one; the other is not content with the legal forms of question and answer unless he holds the other party by the hand. What a shameful admission of the dishonesty and wickedness of mankind! men trust more to our signet-rings than to our intentions. For what are these respectable men summoned? for what do they impress their seals? it is in order that the borrower may not deny that he has received what he has received. You regard these men, I suppose, as above bribes, as maintainers of the truth: well, these very men will not be entrusted with money except on the same terms. Would it not, then, be more honourable to be deceived by some than to suspect all men of dishonesty? To fill up the measure of avarice one thing only is lacking, that we should bestow no benefit without a surety. To help, to be of service, is the part of a generous and noble mind; he who gives acts like a god, he who demands repayment acts like a money-lender. Why then, by trying to protect the rights of the former class, should we reduce them to the level of the basest of mankind?

XVI. "More men," our opponent argues, "will be ungrateful, if no legal remedy exists against ingratitude." Nay, fewer, because then benefits will be bestowed with more discrimination, In the next place, it is not advisable that it should be publicly known how many ungrateful men there are: for the number of sinners will do away with the disgrace of the sin, and a reproach which applies to all men will cease to be dishonourable. Is any woman ashamed of being divorced, now that some noble ladies reckon the years of their lives, not by the number of the consuls, but by that of their husbands, now that they leave their homes in order to marry others, and marry only in order to be divorced? Divorce was only dreaded as long as it was unusual; now that no gazette appears without it, women learn to do what they hear so much about. Can any one feel ashamed of adultery, now that things have come to such a pass that no woman keeps a husband at all unless it be to pique her lover? Chastity merely implies ugliness. Where will you find any woman so abject, so repulsive, as to be satisfied with a single pair of lovers, without having a different one for each hour of the day; nor is the day long enough for all of them, unless she has taken her airing in the grounds of one, and passes the night with another. A woman is frumpish and old-fashioned if she does not know that "adultery with one paramour is nick-named marriage." Just as all shame at these vices has disappeared since the vice itself became so widely spread, so if you made the ungrateful begin to count their own numbers, you would both make them more numerous, and enable them to be ungrateful with greater impunity.

XVII. "What then? shall the ungrateful man go unpunished?" What then, I answer, shall we punish the undutiful, the malicious, the avaricious, the headstrong, and the cruel? Do you imagine that those things which are loathed are not punished, or do you suppose that any punishment is greater than the hate of all men? It is a punishment not to dare receive a benefit from anyone, not to dare to bestow one, to be, or to fancy that you are a mark for all men's eyes, and to lose all appreciation of so excellent and pleasant a matter. Do you call a man unhappy who has lost his sight, or whose hearing has been impaired by disease, and do you not call him wretched who has lost the power of feeling benefits? He fears the gods, the witnesses of all ingratitude; he is tortured by the thought of the benefit which he has misapplied, and, in fine, he is sufficiently punished by this great penalty, that, as I said before, he cannot enjoy the fruits of this most delightful act. On the other hand, he who takes pleasure in receiving a benefit, enjoys an unvarying and continuous happiness, which he derives from consideration, not of the thing given, but of the intention of the giver. A benefit gives perpetual joy to a grateful man, but pleases an ungrateful one only for a moment. Can the lives of such men be compared, seeing that the one is sad and gloomy—as it is natural that a denier of his debts and a defrauder should be, a man who does not give his parents, his nurses, or his teachers the honour which is their due—while the other is joyous, cheerful, on the watch for an opportunity of proving his gratitude, and gaining much pleasure from this frame of mind itself? Such a man has no wish to become bankrupt, but only to make the fullest and most copious return for benefits, and that not only to parents and friends, but also to more humble persons; for even if he receives a benefit from his own slave, he does not consider from whom he receives it, but what he receives.

XVIII. It has, however, been doubted by Hecaton and some other writers, whether a slave can bestow a benefit upon his master. Some distinguish between benefits, duties, and services, calling those things benefits which are bestowed by a stranger—that is, by one who could discontinue them without blame—while duties are performed by our children, our wives, and those whom relationship prompts and orders to afford us help; and, thirdly, services are performed by slaves, whose position is such that nothing which they do for their master can give them any claim upon him....

Besides this, he who affirms that a slave does not sometimes confer a benefit upon his master is ignorant of the rights of man; for the question is, not what the station in life of the giver may be, but what his intentions are. The path of virtue is closed to no one, it lies open to all; it admits and invites all, whether they be free-born men, slaves or freed-men, kings or exiles; it requires no qualifications of family or of property, it is satisfied with a mere man. What, indeed, should we have to trust to for defence against sudden misfortunes, what could—a noble mind promise to itself to keep unshaken, if virtue could be lost together with prosperity? If a slave cannot confer a benefit upon his master, then no subject can confer a benefit upon his king, and no soldier upon his general; for so long as the man is subject to supreme authority, the form of authority can make no difference. If main force, or the fear of death and torture, can prevent a slave from gaining any title to his master's gratitude, they will also prevent the subjects of a king, or the soldiers of a general from doing so, for the same things may happen to either of these classes of men, though under different names.

Yet men do bestow benefits upon their kings and their generals; therefore slaves can bestow benefits upon their masters. A slave can be just, brave, magnanimous; he can therefore bestow a benefit, for this is also the part of a virtuous man. So true is it that slaves can bestow benefits upon their masters, that the masters have often owed their lives to them.

XIX. There is no doubt that a slave can bestow a benefit upon anyone; why, then, not upon his master? "Because," it is argued, "he cannot become his master's creditor if he gives him money. If this be not so, he daily lays his master under an obligation to him; he attends him when on a journey, he nurses him when sick, he works most laboriously at the cultivation of his estate; yet all these, which would be called benefits if done for us by anyone else, are merely called service when done by a slave. A benefit is that which some one bestows who has the option of withholding it:—now a slave has no power to refuse, so that he does not afford us his help, but obeys our orders, and cannot boast of having done what he could not leave undone." Even under these conditions I shall win the day, and will place a slave in such positions, that for many purposes he will be free; in the meanwhile, tell me, if I give you an instance of a slave fighting for his master's safety without regard to himself, pierced through with wounds, yet spending the last drops of his blood, and gaining time for his master to escape by the sacrifice of his life, will you say that this man did not bestow a benefit upon his master because he was a slave? If I give an instance of one who could not be bribed to betray his master's secrets by any of the offers of a tyrant, who was not terrified by any threats, nor overpowered by any tortures, but who, as far as he was able, placed his questioners upon a wrong scent, and, paid for his loyalty with his life; will you say that this man did not confer a benefit upon his master because he was a slave? Consider, rather, whether an example of virtue in a slave be not all the greater because it is rarer than in free men, and whether it be not all the more gratifying that, although to be commanded is odious, and all submission to authority is irksome, yet in some particular cases love for a master has been more powerful than men's general dislike to servitude. A benefit does not, therefore, cease to be a benefit because it is bestowed by a slave, but is all the greater on that account, because not even slavery could restrain him from bestowing it.

XX. It is a mistake to imagine that slavery pervades a man's whole being; the better part of him is exempt from it: the body indeed is subjected and in the power of a master, but the mind is independent, and indeed is so free and wild, that it cannot be restrained even by this prison of the body, wherein it is confined, from following its own impulses, dealing with gigantic designs, and soaring into the infinite, accompanied by all the host of heaven. It is, therefore, only the body which misfortune hands over to a master, and which he buys and sells; this inward part cannot be transferred as a chattel. Whatever comes from this, is free; indeed, we are not allowed to order all things to be done, nor are slaves compelled to obey us in all things; they will not carry out treasonable orders, or lend their hands to an act of crime.

XXI. There are some things which the law neither enjoins nor forbids; it is in these that a slave finds the means of bestowing benefits. As long as we only receive what is generally demanded from a slave, that is mere service; when more is given than a slave need afford us, it is a benefit; as soon as what he does begins to partake of the affection of a friend, it can no longer be called service. There are certain things with which a master is bound to provide his slave, such as food and clothing; no one calls this a benefit; but supposing that he indulges his slave, educates him above his station, teaches him arts which free-born men learn, that is a benefit. The converse is true in the case of the slave; anything which goes beyond the rules of a slave's duty, which is done of his own free will, and not in obedience to orders, is a benefit, provided it be of sufficient importance to be called by such a name if bestowed by any other person.

XXII. It has pleased Chrysippus to define a slave as "a hireling for life." Just as a hireling bestows a benefit when he does more than he engaged himself to do, so when a slave's love for his master raises him above his condition and urges him to do something noble—something which would be a credit even to men more fortunate by birth—he surpasses the hopes of his master, and is a benefit found in the house. Do you think it is just that we should be angry with our slaves when they do less than their duty, and that we should not be grateful to them when they do more? Do you wish to know when their service is not a benefit? When the question can be asked, "What if he had refused to do it?" When he does that which he might have refused to do, we must praise his good will. Benefits and wrongs are opposites; a slave can bestow a benefit upon his master, if he can receive a wrong from his master. Now an official has been appointed to hear complaints of the wrongs done by masters to their slaves, whose duty it is to restrain cruelty and lust, or avarice in providing them with the necessaries of life. What follows, then? Is it the master who receives a benefit from his slave? nay, rather, it is one man who receives it from another. Lastly, he did all that lay in his power; he bestowed a benefit upon his master; it lies in your power to receive or not to receive it from a slave. Yet who is so exalted, that fortune may not make him need the aid even of the lowliest?

XXIII. I shall now quote a number of instances of benefits, not all alike, some even contradictory. Some slaves have given their master life, some death; have saved him when perishing, or, as if that were not enough, have saved him by their own death; others have helped their master to die, some have saved his life by stratagem. Claudius Quadrigarius tells us in the eighteenth book of his "Annals," that when Grumentum was being besieged, and had been reduced to the greatest straits, two slaves deserted to the enemy, and did valuable service. Afterwards, when the city was taken, and the victors were rushing wildly in every direction, they ran before every one else along the streets, which they well knew, to the house in which they had been slaves, and drove their mistress before them; when they were asked who she might be, they answered that she was their mistress, and a most cruel one, and that they were leading her away for punishment. They led her outside the walls, and concealed her with the greatest care until the fighting was over; then, as the soldiery, satisfied with the sack of the city, quickly resumed the manners of Romans, they also returned to their own countrymen, and themselves restored their mistress to them. She manumitted each of them on the spot, and was not ashamed to receive her life from men over whom she had held the power of life and death. She might, indeed, especially congratulate herself upon this; for had she been saved otherwise, she would merely have received a common and hackneyed piece of kindness, whereas, by being saved as she was, she became a glorious legend, and an example to two cities. In the confusion of the captured city, when every one was thinking only of his own safety, all deserted her except these deserters; but they, that they might prove what had been their intentions in effecting that desertion, deserted again from the victors to the captive, wearing the masks of unnatural murderers.

They thought—and this was the greatest part of the service which they rendered—they were content to seem to have murdered their mistress, if thereby their mistress might be saved from murder. Believe me, it is the mark of no slavish soul to purchase a noble deed by the semblance of crime.

When Vettius, the praetor of the Marsi, was being led into the presence of the Roman general, his slave snatched a sword from the soldier who was dragging him along, and first slew his master. Then he said, "It is now time for me to look to myself; I have already set my master free," and with these words transfixed himself with one blow. Can you tell me of anyone who saved his master more gloriously?

XXIV. When Caesar was besieging Corfinium, Domitius, who was shut up in the city, ordered a slave of his own, who was also a physician, to give him poison. Observing the man's hesitation, he said, "Why do you delay, as though the whole business was in your power? I ask for death with arms in my hands." Then the slave assented, and gave him a harmless drug to drink. When Domitius fell asleep after drinking this, the slave went to his son, and said, "Give orders for my being kept in custody until you learn from the result whether I have given your father poison or no." Domitius lived, and Caesar saved his life; but his slave had saved it before.

XXV. During the civil war, a slave hid his master, who had been proscribed, put on his rings and clothes, met the soldiers who were searching for him, and, after declaring that he would not stoop to entreat them not to carry out their orders, offered his neck to their swords. What a noble spirit it shows in a slave to have been willing to die for his master, at a time when few were faithful enough to wish their master to live! to be found kind when the state was cruel, faithful when it was treacherous! to be eager for the reward of fidelity, though it was death, at a time when such rich rewards were offered for treachery!

XXVI. I will not pass over the instances which our own age affords. In the reign of Tiberius Caesar, there was a common and almost universal frenzy for informing, which was more ruinous to the citizens of Rome than the whole civil war; the talk of drunkards, the frankness of jesters, was alike reported to the government; nothing was safe; every opportunity of ferocious punishment was seized, and men no longer waited to hear the fate of accused persons, since it was always the same. One Paulus, of the Praetorian guard, was at an entertainment, wearing a portrait of Tiberius Caesar engraved in relief upon a gem. It would be absurd for me to beat about the bush for some delicate way of explaining that he took up a chamber-pot, an action which was at once noticed by Maro, one of the most notorious informers of that time, and the slave of the man who was about to fall into the trap, who drew the ring from the finger of his drunken master. When Maro called the guests to witness that Paulus had dishonoured the portrait of the emperor, and was already drawing up an act of accusation, the slave showed the ring upon his own finger. Such a man no more deserves to be called a slave, than Maro deserved to be called a guest.

XXVII. In the reign of Augustus men's own words were not yet able to ruin them, yet they sometimes brought them into trouble. A senator named Rufus, while at dinner, expressed a hope that Caesar would not return safe from a journey for which he was preparing, and added that all bulls and calves wished the same thing. Some of those present carefully noted these words. At daybreak, the slave who had stood at his feet during the dinner, told him what he had said in his cups, and urged him to be the first to go to Caesar, and denounce himself. Rufus followed this advice, met Caesar as he was going down to the forum, and, swearing that he was out of his mind the day before, prayed that what he had said might fall upon his own head and that of his children; he then begged Caesar pardon him, and to take him back into favour. When Caesar said that he would do so, he added, "No one will believe that you have taken me back into favour unless you make me a present of something;" and he asked for and obtained a sum of money so large, that it would have been a gift not to be slighted even if bestowed by an unoffended prince. Caesar added: "In future I will take care never to quarrel with you, for my own sake." Caesar acted honourably in pardoning him, and in being liberal as well as forgiving; no one can hear this anecdote without praising Caesar, but he must praise the slave first. You need not wait for me to tell you that the slave who did his master this service was set free; yet his master did not do this for nothing, for Caesar had already paid him the price of the slave's liberty.

XXVIII. After so many instances, can we doubt that a master may sometimes receive a benefit from a slave? Why need the person of the giver detract from the thing which he gives? why should not the gift add rather to the glory of the giver. All men descend from the same original stock; no one is better born than another, except in so far as his disposition is nobler and better suited for the performance of good actions. Those who display portraits of their ancestors in their halls, and set up in the entrance to their houses the pedigree of their family drawn out at length, with many complicated collateral branches, are they not notorious rather than noble? The universe is the one parent of all, whether they trace their descent from this primary source through a glorious or a mean line of ancestors. Be not deceived when men who are reckoning up their genealogy, wherever an illustrious name is wanting, foist in that of a god in its place. You need despise no one, even though he bears a commonplace name, and owes little to fortune. Whether your immediate ancestors were freedmen, or slaves, or foreigners, pluck up your spirits boldly, and leap over any intervening disgraces of your pedigree; at its source, a noble origin awaits you. Why should our pride inflate us to such a degree that we think it beneath us to receive benefits from slaves, and think only of their position, forgetting their good deeds? You, the slave of lust, of gluttony, of a harlot, nay, who are owned as a joint chattel by harlots, can you call anyone else a slave? Call a man a slave? why, I pray you, whither are you being hurried by those bearers who carry your litter? whither are these men with their smart military-looking cloaks carrying you? is it not to the door of some door-keeper, or to the gardens of some one who has not even a subordinate office? and then you, who regard the salute of another man's slave as a benefit, declare that you cannot receive a benefit from your own slave. What inconsistency is this? At the same time you despise and fawn upon slaves, you are haughty and violent at home, while out of doors you are meek, and as much despised as you despise your slaves; for none abase themselves lower than those who unconscionably give themselves airs, nor are anymore prepared to trample upon others than those who have learned how to offer insults by having endured them.

XXIX. I felt it my duty to say this, in order to crush the arrogance of men who are themselves at the mercy of fortune, and to claim the right of bestowing a benefit for slaves, in order that I may claim it also for sons. The question arises, whether children can ever bestow upon their parents greater benefits than those which they have received from them.

It is granted that many sons become greater and more powerful than their parents, and also that they are better men. If this be true, they may give better gifts to their fathers than they have received from them, seeing that their fortune and their good nature are alike greater than that of their father. "Whatever a father receives from his son," our opponent will urge, "must in any case be lees than what the son received from him, because the son owes to his father the very power of giving. Therefore the father can never be surpassed in the bestowal of benefits, because the benefit which surpasses his own is really his." I answer, that some things derive their first origin from others, yet are greater than those others; and a thing may be greater than that from which it took its rise, although without that thing to start from it never could have grown so great. All things greatly outgrow their beginnings. Seeds are the causes of all things, and yet are the smallest part of the things which they produce. Look at the Rhine, or the Euphrates, or any other famous rivers; how small they are, if you only view them at the place from whence they take their rise? they gain all that makes them terrible and renowned as they flow along. Look at the trees which are tallest if you consider their height, and the broadest if you look at their thickness and the spread of their branches; compared with all this, how small a part of them is contained in the slender fibres of the root? Yet take away their roots, and no more groves will arise, nor great mountains be clothed with trees. Temples and cities are supported by their foundations; yet what is built as the foundation of the entire building lies out of sight. So it is in other matters; the subsequent greatness of a thing ever eclipses its origin. I could never have obtained anything without having previously received the boon of existence from my parents; yet it does not follow from this that whatever I obtain is less than that without which I could not obtain it. If my nurse had not fed me when I was a child, I should not have been able to conduct any of those enterprises which I now carry on, both with my head and with my hand, nor should I ever have obtained the fame which is due to my labours both in peace and war; would you on that account argue that the services of a nurse were more valuable than the most important undertakings? Yet is not the nurse as important as the father, since without the benefits which I have received from each of them alike, I should have been alike unable to effect anything? If I owe all that I now can do to my original beginning, I cannot regard my father or my grandfather as being this original beginning; there always will be a spring further back, from which the spring next below is derived. Yet no one will argue that I owe more to unknown and forgotten ancestors than to my father; though really I do owe them more, if I owe it to my ancestors that my father begat me.

XXX. "Whatever I have bestowed upon my father," says my opponent, "however great it may be, yet is less valuable than what my father has bestowed upon me, because if he had not begotten me, it never could have existed at all." By this mode of reasoning, if a man has healed my father when ill, and at the point of death, I shall not be able to bestow anything upon him equivalent to what I have received from him; for had my father not been healed, he could not have begotten me. Yet think whether it be not nearer the truth to regard all that I can do, and all that I have done, as mine, due to my own powers and my own will? Consider what the fact of my birth is in itself; you will see that it is a small matter, the outcome of which is dubious, and that it may lead equally to good or to evil; no doubt it is the first step to everything, but because it is the first, it is not on that account more important than all the others. Suppose that I have saved my father's life, raised him to the highest honours, and made him the chief man in his city, that I have not merely made him illustrious by my own deeds, but have furnished him himself with an opportunity of performing great exploits, which is at once important, easy, and safe, as well as glorious; that I have loaded him with appointments, wealth, and all that attracts men's minds; still, even when I surpass all others, I am inferior to him. Now if you say, "You owe to your father the power of doing all this," I shall answer, "Quite true, if to do all this it is only necessary to be born; but if life is merely an unimportant factor in the art of living well, and if you have bestowed upon me only that which I have in common with wild beasts and the smallest, and some of the foulest of creatures, do not claim for yourself what did not come into being in consequence of the benefits which you bestowed, even though it could not have come into being without them."

XXXI. Suppose, father, that I have saved your life, in return for the life which I received from you: in this case also I have outdone your benefit, because I have given life to one who understands what I have done, and because I understood what I was doing, since I gave you your life not for the sake of, or by the means of my own pleasure; for just as it is less terrible to die before one has time to fear death, so it is a much greater boon to preserve one's life than to receive it. I have given life to one who will at once enjoy it, you gave it to one who knew not if he should ever live; I have given life to one who was in fear of death, your gift of life merely enables me to die; I have given you a life complete, perfect; you begat me without intelligence, a burden upon others. Do you wish to know how far from a benefit it was to give life under such conditions? You should have exposed me as a child, for you did me a wrong in begetting me. What do I gather from this? That the cohabitation of a father and mother is the very least of benefits to their child, unless in addition this beginning of kindnesses be followed up by others, and confirmed by other services. It is not a good thing to live, but to live well. "But," say you, "I do live well." True, but I might have lived ill; so that your part in me is merely this, that I live. If you claim merit to yourself for giving me mere life, bare and helpless, and boast of it as a great boon, reflect that this you claim merit for giving me is a boon which I possess in common with flies and worms. In the next place, if I say no more than that I have applied myself to honourable pursuits, and have guided the course of my life along the path of rectitude, then you have received more from your benefit than you gave; for you gave me to myself ignorant and unlearned, and I have returned to you a son such as you would wish to have begotten.

XXXII. My father supported me. If I repay this kindness, I give him more than I received, because he has the pleasure, not only of being supported, but of being supported by a son, and receives more delight from my filial devotion than from the food itself, whereas the food which he used to give me merely affected my body. What? if any man rises so high as to become famous among nations for his eloquence, his justice, or his military skill, if much of the splendour of his renown is shed upon his father also, and by its clear light dispels the obscurity of his birth, does not such a man confer an inestimable benefit upon his parents? Would anyone have heard of Aristo and Gryllus except through Xenophon and Plato, their sons? Socrates keeps alive the memory of Sophroniscus. It would take long to recount the other men whose names survive for no other reason than that the admirable qualities of their sons have handed them down to posterity. Did the father of Marcus Agrippa, of whom nothing was known, even after Agrippa became famous, confer the greater benefit upon his son, or was that greater which Agrippa conferred upon his father when he gained the glory, unique in the annals of war, of a naval crown, and when he raised so many vast buildings in Rome, which not only surpassed all former grandeur, but have been surpassed by none since? Did Octavius confer a greater benefit upon his son, or the Emperor Augustus upon his father, obscured as he was by the intervention of an adoptive father? What joy would he have experienced, if, after the putting down of the civil war, he had seen his son ruling the state in peace and security? He would not have recognized the good which he had himself bestowed, and would hardly have believed, when he looked back upon himself, that so great a man could have been born in his house. Why should I go on to speak of others who would now be forgotten, if the glory of their sons had not raised them from obscurity, and kept them in the light until this day? In the next place, as we are not considering what son may have given back to his father greater benefits than he received from him, but whether a son can give back greater benefits, even if the examples which I have quoted are not sufficient, and such benefits do not outweigh the benefits bestowed by the parents, if no age has produced. an actual example, still it is not in the nature of things impossible. Though no solitary act can outweigh the deserts of a parent, yet many such acts combined by one son may do so.

XXXIII. Scipio, while under seventeen years of age, rode

among the enemy in battle, and saved his father's life. Was it not enough, that in order to reach his father he despised so many dangers when they were pressing hardest upon the greatest generals, that he, a novice in his first battle, made his way through so many obstacles, over the bodies of so many veteran soldiers, and showed strength and courage beyond his years? Add to this, that he also defended his father in court, and saved him from a plot of his powerful enemies, that he heaped upon him a second and a third consulship and other posts which were coveted even by consulars, that when his father was poor he bestowed upon him the plunder which he took by military licence, and that he made him rich with the spoils of the enemy, which is the greatest honour of a soldier. If even this did not repay his debt, add to it that he caused him to be constantly employed in the government of provinces and in special commands, add, that after he had destroyed the greatest cities, and became without a rival either in the east or in the west, the acknowledged protector and second founder of the Roman Empire, he bestowed upon one who was already of noble birth the higher title of "the father of Scipio;" can we doubt that the commonplace benefit of his birth was outdone by his exemplary conduct, and by the valour which was at once the glory and the protection of his country? Next, if this be not enough, suppose that a son were to rescue his father from the torture, or to undergo it in his stead. You can suppose the benefits returned by the son as great as you please, whereas the gift he received from his father was of one sort only, was easily performed, and was a pleasure to the giver; that he must necessarily have given the same thing to many others, even to some to whom he knows not that he has given it, that he had a partner in doing so, and that he had in view the law, patriotism, the rewards bestowed upon fathers of families by the state, the maintenance of his house and family: everything rather than him to whom he was giving life. What? supposing that any one were to learn philosophy and teach it to his father, could it be any longer disputed that the son had given him something greater than he had received from him, having returned to his father a happy life, whereas he had received from him merely life?

XXXIV. "But," says our opponent, "whatever you do, whatever you are able to give to your father, is part of his benefit bestowed upon you." So it is the benefit of my teacher that I have become proficient in liberal studies; yet we pass on from those who taught them to us, at any rate from those who taught us the alphabet; and although no one can learn anything without them, yet it does not follow that whatsoever success one subsequently obtains, one is still inferior to those teachers. There is a great difference between the beginning of a thing and its final development; the beginning is not equal to the thing at its greatest, merely upon the ground that, without the beginning, it could never have become so great.

XXXV. It is now time for me to bring forth something, so to speak, from my own mint. So long as there is something better than the benefit which a man bestows, he may be outdone. A father gives life to his son; there is something better than life; therefore a father may be outdone, because there is something better than the benefit which he has bestowed. Still further, he who has given any one his life, if he be more than once saved from peril of death by him, has received a greater benefit than he bestowed. Now, a father has given life to his son: if, therefore, he be more than once saved from peril by his son, he can receive a greater benefit than he gave. A benefit becomes greater to the receiver in proportion to his need of it. Now he who is alive needs life more than he who has not been born, seeing that such a one can have no need at all; consequently a father, if his life is saved by his son, receives a greater benefit than his son received from him by being born. It is said, "The benefits conferred by fathers cannot be outdone by those returned by their sons." Why? "Because the son received life from his father, and had he not received it, he could not have returned any benefits at all." A father has this in common with all those who have given any men their lives; it is impossible that these men could repay the debt if they had not received their life. Then I suppose one cannot overpay one's debt to a physician, for a physician gives life as well as a father; or to a sailor who has saved us when shipwrecked? Yet the benefits bestowed by these and by all the others who give us life in whatever fashion, can be outdone: consequently those of our fathers can be outdone. If any one bestows upon me a benefit which requires the help of benefits from many other persons, whereas I give him what requires no one to help it out, I have given more than I have received; now a father gave to his son a life which, without many accessories to preserve it, would perish; whereas a son, if he gives life to his father, gives him a life which requires no assistance to make it lasting; therefore the father who receives life from his son, receives a greater benefit than he himself bestowed upon his son.

XXXVI. These considerations do not destroy the respect due to parents, or make their children behave worse to them, nay, better; for virtue is naturally ambitious, and wishes to outstrip those who are before it. Filial piety will be all the more eager, if, in returning a father's benefits, it can hope to outdo them; nor will this be against the will or the pleasure of the father, since in many contests it is to our advantage to be outdone. How does this contest become so desirable? How comes it to be such happiness to parents that they should confess themselves outdone by the benefits bestowed by their children? Unless we decide the matter thus, we give children an excuse, and make them less eager to repay their debt, whereas we ought to spur them on, saying, "Noble youths, give your attention to this! You are invited to contend in an honourable strife between parents and children, as to which party has received more than it has given. Your fathers have not necessarily won the day because they are first in the field: only take courage, as befits you, and do not give up the contest; you will conquer if you wish to do so. In this honourable warfare you will have no lack of leaders who will encourage you to perform deeds like their own, and bid you follow in their footsteps upon a path by which victory has often before now been won over parents."

XXXVII. AEneas conquered his father in well doing, for he himself had been but a light and a safe burden for him when he was a child, yet he bore his father, when heavy with age, through the midst of the enemy's lines and the crash of the city which was falling around him, albeit the devout old man, who bore the sacred images and the household gods in his hands, pressed him with more than his own weight; nevertheless (what cannot filial piety accomplish!) AEneas bore him safe through the blazing city, and placed him in safety, to be worshipped as one of the founders of the Roman Empire. Those Sicilian youths outdid their parents whom they bore away safe, when Aetna, roused to unusual fury, poured fire over cities and fields throughout a great part of the island. It is believed that the fires parted, and that the flames retired on either side, so as to leave a passage for these youths to pass through, who certainly deserved to perform their daring task in safety. Antigonus outdid his father when, after having conquered the enemy in a great battle, he transferred the fruits of it to him, and handed over to him the empire of Cyprus. This is true kingship, to choose not to be a king when you might. Manlius conquered his father, imperious [Footnote: There is an allusion to the surname of both the father and the son, "Imperiosus" given them on account of their severity.] though he was, when, in spite of his having previously been banished for a time by his father on, account of his dulness and stupidity as a boy, he came to an interview which he had demanded with the tribune of the people, who had filed an action against his father. The tribune had granted him the interview, hoping that he would betray his hated father, and believed that he had earned the gratitude of the youth, having, amongst other matters, reproached old Manlius with sending him into exile, treating it as a very serious accusation; but the youth, having caught him alone, drew a sword which he had hidden in his robe, and said, "Unless you swear to give up your suit against my father, I will run you through with this sword. It is in your power to decide how my father shall be freed from his prosecutor." The tribune swore, and kept his oath; he related the reason of his abandonment of his action to an assembly at the Rostra. No other man was ever permitted to put down a tribune with impunity.

XXXVIII. There are instances without number of men who have saved their parents from danger, have raised them from the lowest to the highest station, and, taking them from the nameless mass of the lower classes, have given them a name glorious throughout all ages. By no force of words, by no power of genius, can one rightly express how desirable, how admirable, how never to be erased from human memory it is to be able to say, "I obeyed my parents, I gave way to them, I was submissive to their authority whether it was just, or unjust and harsh; the only point in which I resisted them was, not to be conquered by them in benefits." Continue this struggle, I beg of you, and even though weary, yet re-form your ranks. Happy are they who conquer, happy they who are conquered. What can be more glorious than the youth who can say to himself—it would not be right to say it to another—"I have conquered my father with benefits"?

What is more fortunate than that old man who declares everywhere to everyone that he has been conquered in benefits by his son? What, again, is more blissful than to be overcome in such a contest?

BOOK IV.

I.

Of all the matters which we have discussed, Aebutius Liberalis, there is none more essential, or which, as Sallust says, ought to be stated with more care than that which is now before us: whether the bestowal of benefits and the return of gratitude for them are desirable objects in themselves. Some men are found who act honourably from commercial motives, and who do not care for unrewarded virtue, though it can confer no glory if it brings any profit. What can be more base than for a man to consider what it costs him to be a good man, when virtue neither allures by gain nor deters by loss, and is so far from bribing any one with hopes and promises, that on the other hand she bids them spend money upon herself, and often consists in voluntary gifts? We must go to her, trampling what is merely useful under our feet: whithersoever she may call us or send us we must go, without any regard for our private fortunes, sometimes without sparing even our own blood, nor must we ever refuse to obey any of her commands. "What shall I gain," says my opponent, "if I do this bravely and gratefully?" You will gain the doing of it—the deed itself is your gain. Nothing beyond this is promised. If any advantage chances to accrue to you, count it as something extra. The reward of honourable dealings lies in themselves. If honour is to be sought after for itself, since a benefit is honourable, it follows that because both of these are of the same nature, their conditions must also be the same. Now it has frequently and satisfactorily been proved, that honour ought to be sought after for itself alone.

II. In this part of the subject we oppose the Epicureans, an effeminate and dreamy sect who philosophize in their own paradise, amongst whom virtue is the handmaid of pleasures, obeys them, is subject to them, and regards them as superior to itself. You say, "there is no pleasure without virtue." But wherefore is it superior to virtue? Do you imagine that the matter in dispute between them is merely one of precedence? Nay, it is virtue itself and its powers which are in question. It cannot be virtue if it can follow; the place of virtue is first, she ought to lead, to command, to stand in the highest rank; you bid her look for a cue to follow. "What," asks our opponent, "does that matter to you? I also declare that happiness is impossible without virtue. Without virtue I disapprove of and condemn the very pleasures which I pursue, and to which I have surrendered myself. The only matter in dispute is this, whether virtue be the cause of the highest good, or whether it be itself the highest good." Do you suppose, though this be the only point in question, that it is a mere matter of precedence? It is a confusion and obvious blindness to prefer the last to the first. I am not angry at virtue being placed below pleasure, but at her being mixed up at all with pleasure, which she despises, whose enemy she is, and from which she separates herself as far as possible, being more at home with labour and sorrow, which are manly troubles, than with your womanish good things.

III. It was necessary to insert this argument, my Liberalis, because it is the part of virtue to bestow those benefits which we are now discussing, and it is most disgraceful to bestow benefits for any other purpose than that they should be free gifts. If we give with the hope of receiving a return, we should give to the richest men, not to the most deserving: whereas we prefer a virtuous poor man to an unmannerly rich one. That is not a benefit, which takes into consideration the fortune of the receiver. Moreover, if our only motive for benefiting others was our own advantage, those who could most easily distribute benefits, such as rich and powerful men, or kings, and persons who do not stand in need of the help of others, ought never to do so at all; the gods would not bestow upon us the countless blessings which they pour upon us unceasingly by night and by day, for their own nature suffices them in all respects, and renders them complete, safe, and beyond the reach of harm; they will, therefore, never bestow a benefit upon any one, if self and self interest be the only cause for the bestowal of benefits. To take thought, not where your benefit will be best bestowed, but where it may be most profitably placed at interest, from whence you will most easily get it back, is not bestowal of benefits, but usury. Now the gods have nothing to do with usury; it follows, therefore, that they cannot be liberal; for if the only reason for giving is the advantage of the giver, since God cannot hope to receive any advantages from us, there is no cause why God should give anything.

IV. I know what answer may be made to this. "True; therefore God does not bestow benefits, but, free from care and unmindful of us, He turns away from our world and either does something else, or else does nothing, which Epicurus thought the greatest possible happiness, and He is not affected either by benefits or by injuries." The man who says this cannot surely hear the voices of worshippers, and of those who all around him are raising their hands to heaven and praying for the success both of their private affairs and those of the state; which certainly would not be the case, all men would not agree in this madness of appealing to deaf and helpless gods, unless we knew that their benefits are sometimes bestowed upon us unasked, sometimes in answer to our prayers, and that they give us both great and seasonable gifts, which shield us from the most terrible dangers. Who is there so poor, so uncared for, born to sorrow by so unkind a fate, as never to have felt the vast generosity of the Gods? Look even at those who complain and are discontented with their lot; you will find that they are not altogether without a share in the bounty of heaven, that there is no one upon whom something has not been shed from that most gracious fount. Is the gift which is bestowed upon all alike, at their birth, not enough? However unequally the blessings of after life may be dealt out to us, did nature give us too little when she gave us herself?

V. It is said, "God does not bestow benefits." Whence, then, comes all that you possess, that you give or refuse to give, that you hoard or steal? whence come these innumerable delights of our eyes, our ears, and our minds? whence the plenty which provides us even with luxury—for it is not our bare necessities alone against which provision is made; we are loved so much as actually to be pampered—whence so many trees bearing various fruits, so many wholesome herbs, so many different sorts of food distributed throughout the year, so that even the slothful may find sustenance in the chance produce of the earth? Then, too, whence come the living creatures of all kinds, some inhabiting the dry land, others the waters, others alighting from the sky, that every part of nature may pay us some tribute; the rivers which encircle our meadows with most beauteous bends, the others which afford a passage to merchant fleets as they flow on, wide and navigable, some of which in summer time are subject to extraordinary overflowings in order that lands lying parched under a glowing sun may suddenly be watered by the rush of a midsummer torrent?

What of the fountains of medicinal waters? What of the bursting forth of warm waters upon the seashore itself? Shall I

"Tell of the seas round Italy that flow,
Which laves her shore above, and which below;
Or of her lakes, unrivalled Larius, thee,
Or thee, Benacus, roaring like a sea?"

VI. If any one gave you a few acres, you would say that you had received a benefit; can you deny that the boundless extent of the earth is a benefit? If any one gave you money, and filled your chest, since you think that so important, you would call that a benefit. God has buried countless mines in the earth, has poured out from the earth countless rivers, rolling sands of gold; He has concealed in every place huge masses of silver, copper and iron, and has bestowed upon you the means of discovering them, placing upon the surface of the earth signs of the treasures hidden below; and yet do you say that you have received no benefit? If a house were given you, bright with marble, its roof beautifully painted with colours and gilding, you would call it no small benefit. God has built for you a huge mansion that fears no fire or ruin, in which you see no flimsy veneers, thinner than the very saw with which they are cut, but vast blocks of most precious stone, all composed of those various and different substances whose paltriest fragments you admire so much; he has built a roof which glitters in one fashion by day, and in another by night; and yet do you say that you have received no benefit? When you so greatly prize what you possess, do you act the part of an ungrateful man, and think that there is no one to whom you are indebted for them? Whence comes the breath which you draw? the light by which you arrange and perform all the actions of your life? the blood by whose circulation your vital warmth is maintained? those meats which excite your palate by their delicate flavour after your hunger is appeased? those provocatives which rouse you when wearied with pleasure? that repose in which you are rotting and mouldering? Will you not, if you are grateful, say—

"'Tis to a god that this repose I owe,
For him I worship, as a god below.
Oft on his altar shall my firstlings bleed,
See, by his bounty here with rustic reed
I play the airs I love the livelong day,
The while my oxen round about me stray."

The true God is he who has placed, not a few oxen, but all the herds on their pastures throughout the world; who furnishes food to the flocks wherever they wander; who has ordained the alternation of summer and winter pasturage, and has taught us not merely to play upon a reed, and to reduce to some order a rustic and artless song, but who has invented so many arts and varieties of voice, so many notes to make music, some with our own breath, some with instruments. You cannot call our inventions our own any more than you call our growth our own, or the various bodily functions which correspond to each stage of our lives; at one time comes the loss of childhood's teeth, at another, when our age is advancing and growing into robuster manhood, puberty and the last wisdom-tooth marks the end of our youth. "We have implanted in us the seeds of all ages, of all arts, and God our master brings forth our intellects from obscurity."

VII. "Nature," says my opponent, "gives me all this." Do you not perceive when you say this that you merely speak of God under another name? for what is nature but God and divine reason, which pervades the universe and all its parts? You may address the author of our world by as many different titles as you please; you may rightly call him Jupiter, Best and Greatest, and the Thunderer, or the Stayer, so called, not because, as the historians tell us, he stayed the flight of the Roman army in answer to the prayer of Romulus, but because all things continue in their stay through his goodness. If you were to call this same personage Fate, you would not lie; for since fate is nothing more than a connected chain of causes, he is the first cause of all upon which all the rest depend. You will also be right in applying to him any names that you please which express supernatural strength and power: he may have as many titles as he has attributes.

VIII. Our school regards him as Father Liber, and Hercules, and Mercurius: he is Father Liber because he is the parent of all, who first discovered the power of seed, and our being led by pleasure to plant it; he is Hercules, because his might is unconquered, and when it is wearied after completing its labours, will retire into fire; he is Mercurius, because in him is reasoning, and numbers, and system, and knowledge. Whither-soever you turn yourself you will see him meeting you: nothing is void of him, he himself fills his own work. Therefore, most ungrateful of mortals, it is in vain that you declare yourself indebted, not to God, but to nature, because there can be no God without nature, nor any nature without God; they are both the same thing, differing only in their functions. If you were to say that you owe to Annaeus or to Lucius what you received from Seneca, you would not change your creditor, but only his name, because he remains the same man whether you use his first, second, or third name. So whether you speak of nature, fate, or fortune, these are all names of the same God, using his power in different ways. So likewise justice, honesty, discretion, courage, frugality, are all the good qualities of one and the same mind; if you are pleased with any one of these, you are pleased with that mind.

IX. However, not to drift aside into a distinct controversy, God bestows upon us very many and very great benefits without hope of receiving any return; since he does not require any offering from us, and we are not capable of bestowing anything upon him: wherefore, a benefit is desirable in itself. In it the advantage of the receiver is all that is taken into consideration: we study this without regarding our own interests. "Yet," argues our opponent, "you say that we ought to choose with care the persons upon whom we bestow benefits, because neither do husbandmen sow seed in the sand: now if this be true, we follow our own interest in bestowing benefits, just as much as in ploughing and sowing: for sowing is not desirable in itself. Besides this you inquire where and how you ought to bestow a benefit, which would not need to be done if the bestowal of a benefit was desirable in itself: because in whatever place and whatever manner it might be bestowed, it still would be a benefit." We seek to do honourable acts, solely because they are honourable; yet even though we need think of nothing else, we consider to whom we shall do them, and when, and how; for in these points the act has its being. In like manner, when I choose upon whom I shall bestow a benefit, and when I aim at making it a benefit; because if it were bestowed upon a base person, it could neither be a benefit nor an honourable action.

X. To restore what has been entrusted to one is desirable in itself; yet I shall not always restore it, nor shall I do so in any place or at any time you please. Sometimes it makes no difference whether I deny that I have received it, or return it openly. I shall consider the interests of the person to whom I am to return it, and shall deny that I have received a deposit, which would injure him if returned. I shall act in the same manner in bestowing a benefit: I shall consider when to give it, to whom, in what manner, and on what grounds. Nothing ought to be done without a reason: a benefit is not truly so, if it be bestowed without a reason, since reason accompanies all honorable action. How often do we hear men reproaching themselves for some thoughtless gift, and saying, "I had rather have thrown it away than have given it to him!" What is thoughtlessly given away is lost in the most discreditable manner, and it is much worse to have bestowed a benefit badly than to have received no return for it; that we receive no return is the fault of another; that we did not choose upon whom we should bestow it, is our own. In choosing a fit person, I shall not, as you expect, pay the least attention to whether I am likely to get any return from him, for I choose one who will be grateful, not one who will return my goodness, and it often happens that the man who makes no return is grateful, while he who returns a benefit is ungrateful for it. I value men by their hearts alone, and, therefore, I shall pass over a rich man if he be unworthy, and give to a good man though he be poor; for he will be grateful however destitute he may be, since whatever he may lose, his heart will still be left him.

XI. I do not fish for gain, for pleasure, or for credit, by bestowing benefits: satisfied in doing so with pleasing one man alone, I shall give in order to do my duty. Duty, however, leaves one some choice; do you ask me, how I am to choose? I shall choose an honest, plain, man, with a good memory, and grateful for kindness; one who keeps his hands off other men's goods, yet does not greedily hold to his own, and who is kind to others; when I have chosen such a man, I shall have acted to my mind, although fortune may have bestowed upon him no means of returning my kindness. If my own advantage and mean calculation made me liberal, if I did no one any service except in order that he might in turn do a service to me, I should never bestow a benefit upon one who was setting out for distant and foreign countries, never to return; I should not bestow a benefit upon one who was so ill as to be past hope of recovery, nor should I do so when I myself was failing, because I should not live long enough to receive any return. Yet, that you may know that to do good is desirable in itself, we afford help to strangers who put into our harbour only to leave it straightway; we give a ship and fit it out for a shipwrecked stranger to sail back in to his own country. He leaves us hardly knowing who it was who saved him, and, as he will never return to our presence, he hands over his debt of gratitude to the gods, and beseeches them to fulfil it for him: in the meanwhile we rejoice in the barren knowledge that we have done a good action. What? when we stand upon the extreme verge of life, and make our wills, do we not assign to others benefits from which we ourselves shall receive no advantage? How much time we waste, how long we consider in secret how much property we are to leave, and to whom! What then? does it make any difference to us to whom we leave our property, seeing that we cannot expect any return from any one? Yet we never give anything with more care, we never take such pains in deciding upon our verdict, as when, without any views of personal advantage, we think only of what is honourable, for we are bad judges of our duty as long as our view of it is distorted by hope and fear, and that most indolent of vices, pleasure: but when death has shut off all these, and brought us as incorrupt judges to pronounce sentence, we seek for the most worthy men to leave our property to, and we never take more scrupulous care than in deciding what is to be done with what does not concern us. Yet, by Hercules, then there steals over us a great satisfaction as we think, "I shall make this man richer, and by bestowing wealth upon that man I shall add lustre to his high position." Indeed, if we never give without expecting some return, we must all die without making our wills.

XII. It may be said, "You define a benefit as a loan which cannot be repaid: now a loan is not a desirable thing in itself." When we speak of a loan, we make use of a figure, or comparison, just as we speak of law as; the standard of right and wrong, although a standard is not a thing to be desired for its own sake. I have adopted this phrase in order to illustrate my subject: when I speak of a loan, I must be understood to mean something resembling a loan. Do you wish to know how it differs from one? I add the words "which cannot be repaid," whereas every loan both can and ought to be repaid. It is so far from being right to bestow a benefit for one's own advantage, that often, as I have explained, it is one's duty to bestow it when it involves one's own loss and risk: for instance, if I assist a man when beset by robbers, so that he gets away from them safely, or help some victim of power, and bring upon myself the party spite of a body of influential men, very, probably incurring myself the same disgrace from which I saved him, although I might have taken the other side, and looked on with safety at struggles with which I have nothing to do: if I were to give bail for one who has been condemned, and when my friend's goods were advertised for sale I were to give a bond to the effect that I would make restitution to the creditors, if, in order to save a proscribed person I myself run the risk of being proscribed. No one, when about to buy a villa at Tusculum or Tibur, for a summer retreat, because of the health of the locality, considers how many years' purchase he gives for it; this must be looked to by the man who makes a profit by it. The same is true with benefits; when you ask what return I get for them, I answer, the consciousness of a good action. "What return does one get for benefits?" Pray tell me what return one gets for righteousness, innocence, magnanimity, chastity, temperance? If you wish for anything beyond these virtues, you do not wish for the virtues themselves. For what does the order of the universe bring round the seasons? for what does the sun make the day now longer and now shorter? all these things are benefits, for they take place for our good. As it is the duty of the universe to maintain the round of the seasons, as it is the duty of the sun to vary the points of his rising and setting, and to do all these things by which we profit, without any reward, so is it the duty of man, amongst other things, to bestow benefits. Wherefore then does he give? He gives for fear that he should not give, lest he might lose an opportunity of doing a good action.

XIII. You Epicureans take pleasure in making a study of dull torpidity, in seeking for a repose which differs little from sound sleep, in lurking beneath the thickest shade, in amusing with the feeblest possible trains of thought that sluggish condition of your languid minds which you term tranquil contemplation, and in stuffing with food and drink, in the recesses of your gardens, your bodies which are pallid with want of exercise; we Stoics, on the other hand, take pleasure in bestowing benefits, even though they cost us labour, provided that they lighten the labours of others; though they lead us into danger, provided that they save others, though they straiten our means, if they alleviate the poverty and distresses of others. What difference does it make to me whether I receive benefits or not? even if I receive them, it is still my duty to bestow them. A benefit has in view the advantage of him upon whom we bestow it, not our own; otherwise we merely bestow it upon ourselves. Many things, therefore, which are of the greatest possible use to others lose all claim to gratitude by being paid for. Merchants are of use to cities, physicians to invalids, dealers to slaves; yet all these have no claim to the gratitude of those whom they benefit, because they seek their own advantage through that of others. That which is bestowed with a view to profit is not a benefit. "I will give this in order that I may get a return for it" is the language of a broker.

XIV. I should not call a woman modest, if she rebuffed her lover in order to increase his passion, or because she feared the law or her husband; as Ovid says:

"She that denies, because she does not dare
To yield, in spirit grants her lover's prayer."

Indeed, the woman who owes her chastity, not to her own virtue, but to fear, may rightly be classed as a sinner. In the same manner, he who merely gave in order that he might receive, cannot be said to have given. Pray, do we bestow benefits upon animals when we feed them for our use or for our table? do we bestow benefits upon trees when we tend them that they may not suffer from drought or from hardness of ground? No one is moved by righteousness and goodness of heart to cultivate an estate, or to do any act in which the reward is something apart from the act itself; but he is moved to bestow benefits, not by low and grasping motives, but by a kind and generous mind, which even after it has given is willing to give again, to renew its former bounties by fresh ones, which thinks only of how much good it can do the man to whom it gives; whereas to do any one a service because it is our interest to do so is a mean action, which deserves no praise, no credit. What grandeur is there in loving oneself, sparing oneself, gaining profit for oneself? The true love of giving calls us away from all this, forcibly leads us to put up with loss, and foregoes its own interest, deriving its greatest pleasure from the mere act of doing good.

XV. Can we doubt that the converse of a benefit is an injury? As the infliction of injuries is a thing to be avoided, so is the bestowal of benefits to be desired for its own sake. In the former, the disgrace of crime outweighs all the advantages which incite us to commit it; while we are urged to the latter course by the appearance of honour, in itself a powerful incentive to action, which attends it.

I should not lie if I were to affirm that every one takes pleasure in the benefits which he has bestowed, that everyone loves best to see the man whom he has most largely benefited. Who does not thinks that to have bestowed one benefit is a reason for bestowing a second? and would this be so, if the act of giving did not itself give us pleasure? How often you may hear a man say, "I cannot bear to desert one whose life I have preserved, whom I have saved from danger. True, he asks me to plead his cause against men of great influence. I do not wish to do so, yet what am I to do? I have already helped him once, nay twice." Do you not perceive how very powerful this instinct must be, if it leads us to bestow benefits first because it is right to do so, and afterwards because we have already bestowed somewhat? Though at the outset a man may have had no claim upon us, we yet continue to give to him because we have already given to him. So untrue is it that we are urged to bestow benefits by our own interest, that even when our benefits prove failures we continue to nurse them and encourage them out of sheer love of benefiting, which has a natural weakness even for what has been ill-bestowed, like that which we feel for our vicious children.

XVI. These same adversaries of ours admit that they are grateful, yet not because it is honourable, but because it is profitable to be so. This can be proved to be untrue all the more easily, because it can be established by the same arguments by which we have established that to bestow a benefit is desirable for its own sake. All our arguments start from this settled point, that honour is pursued for no reason except because it is honour.

Now, who will venture to raise the question whether it be honourable to be grateful? who does not loathe the ungrateful man, useless as he is even to himself? How do you feel when any one is spoken of as being ungrateful for great benefits conferred upon him by a friend? Is it as though he had done something base, or had merely neglected to do something useful and likely to be profitable to himself? I imagine that you think him a bad man, and one who deserves punishment, not one who needs a guardian; and this would not be the case, unless gratitude were desirable in itself and honourable. Other qualities, it may be, manifest their importance less clearly, and require an explanation to prove whether they be honourable or no; this is openly proved to be so in the sight of all, and is too beautiful for anything to obscure or dim its glory. What is more praiseworthy, upon what are all men more universally agreed, than to return gratitude for good offices?

XVII. Pray tell me, what is it that urges us to do so? Is it profit? Why, unless a man despises profit, he is not grateful. Is it ambition? why, what is there to boast of in having paid what you owe? Is it fear? The ungrateful man feels none, for against this one crime we have provided no law, as though nature had taken sufficient precautions against it. Just as there is no law which bids parents love and indulge their children, seeing that it is superfluous to force us into the path which we naturally take, just as no one needs to be urged to love himself, since self-love begins to act upon him as soon as he is born, so there is no law bidding us to seek that which is honourable in itself; for such things please us by their very nature, and so attractive is virtue that the disposition even of bad men leads them to approve of good rather than of evil. Who is there who does not wish to appear beneficent, who does not even when steeped in crime and wrong-doing strive after the appearance of goodness, does not put some show of justice upon even his most intemperate acts, and endeavour to seem to have conferred a benefit even upon those whom he has injured? Consequently, men allow themselves to be thanked by those whom they have ruined, and pretend to be good and generous, because they cannot prove themselves so; and this they never would do were it not that a love of honour for its own sake forces them to seek a reputation quite at variance with their real character, and to conceal their baseness, a quality whose fruits we covet, though we regard it itself with dislike and shame. No one has ever so far rebelled against the laws of nature and put off human feeling as to act basely for mere amusement. Ask any of those who live by robbery whether he would not rather obtain what he steals and plunders by honest means; the man whose trade is highway robbery and the murder of travellers would rather find his booty than take it by force; you will find no one who would not prefer to enjoy the fruits of wickedness without acting wickedly. Nature bestows upon us all this immense advantage, that the light of virtue shines into the minds of all alike; even those who do not follow her, behold her.

XVIII. A proof that gratitude is desirable for itself lies in the fact that ingratitude is to be avoided for itself, because no vice more powerfully rends asunder and destroys the union of the human race. To what do we trust for safety, if not in mutual good offices one to another? It is by the interchange of benefits alone that we gain some measure of protection for our lives, and of safety against sudden disasters. Taken singly, what should we be? a prey and quarry for wild beasts, a luscious and easy banquet; for while all other animals have sufficient strength to protect themselves, and those which are born to a wandering solitary life are armed, man is covered by a soft skin, has no powerful teeth or claws with which to terrify other creatures, but weak and naked by himself is made strong by union.

God has bestowed upon him two gifts, reason and union, which raise him from weakness to the highest power; and so he, who if taken alone would be inferior to every other creature, possesses supreme dominion. Union has given him sovereignty over all animals; union has enabled a being born upon the earth to assume power over a foreign element, and bids him be lord of the sea also; it is union which has checked the inroads of disease, provided supports for our old age, and given us relief from pain; it is union which makes us strong, and to which we look for protection against the caprices of fortune. Take away union, and you will rend asunder the association by which the human race preserves its existence; yet you will take it away if you succeed in proving that ingratitude is not to be avoided for itself, but because something is to be feared for it; for how many are there who can with safety be ungrateful? In fine, I call every man ungrateful who is merely made grateful by fear.

XIX. No sane man fears the gods; for it is madness to fear what is beneficial, and no man loves those whom he fears. You, Epicurus, ended by making God unarmed; you stripped him of all weapons, of all power, and, lest anyone should fear him, you banished him out of the world. There is no reason why you should fear this being, cut off as he is, and separated from the sight and touch of mortals by a vast and impassable wall; he has no power either of rewarding or of injuring us; he dwells alone half-way between our heaven and that of another world, without the society either of animals, of men, or of matter, avoiding the crash of worlds as they fall in ruins above and around him, but neither hearing our prayers nor interested in us. Yet you wish to seem to worship this being just as a father, with a mind, I suppose, full of gratitude; or, if you do not wish to seem grateful, why should you worship him, since you have received no benefit from him, but have been put together entirely at random and by chance by those atoms and mites of yours? "I worship him," you answer, "because of his glorious majesty and his unique nature." Granting that you do this, you clearly do it without the attraction of any reward, or any hope; there is therefore something which is desirable for itself, whose own worth attracts you, that is, honour. Now what is more honourable than gratitude? the means of practising this virtue are as extensive as life itself.

XX. "Yet," argues he, "there is also a certain amount of profit inherent in this virtue." In what virtue is there not? But that which we speak of as desirable for itself is such, that although it may possess some attendant advantages, yet it would be desirable even if stripped of all these. It is profitable to be grateful; yet I will be grateful even though it harm me. What is the aim of the grateful man? is it that his gratitude may win for him more friends and more benefits? What then? If a man is likely to meet with affronts by showing his gratitude, if he knows that far from gaining anything by it, he must lose much even of what he has already acquired, will he not cheerfully act to his own disadvantage? That man is ungrateful who, in returning a kindness, looks forward to a second gift—who hopes while he repays. I call him ungrateful who sits at the bedside of a sick man because he is about to make a will, when he is at leisure to think of inheritances and legacies. Though he may do everything which a good and dutiful friend ought to do, yet, if any hope of gain be floating in his mind, he is a mere legacy-hunter, and is angling for an inheritance. Like the birds which feed upon carcases, which come close to animals weakened by disease, and watch till they fall, so these men are attracted by death and hover around a corpse.

XXI. A grateful mind is attracted only by a sense of the beauty of its purpose. Do you wish to know this to be so, and that it is not bribed by ideas of profit? There are two classes of grateful men: a man is called grateful who has made some return for what he received; this man may very possibly display himself in this character, he has something to boast of, to refer to. We also call a man grateful who receives a benefit with goodwill, and owes it to his benefactor with goodwill; yet this man's gratitude lies concealed within his own mind. What profit can accrue to him from this latent feeling? yet this man, even though he is not able to do anything more than this, is grateful; he loves his benefactor, he feels his debt to him, he longs to repay his kindness; whatever else you may find wanting, there is nothing wanting in the man. He is like a workman who has not the tools necessary for the practice of his craft, or like a trained singer whose voice cannot be heard through the noise of those who interrupt him. I wish to repay a kindness: after this there still remains something for me to do, not in order that I may become grateful, but that I may discharge my debt; for, in many cases, he who returns a kindness is ungrateful for it, and he who does not return it is grateful. Like all other virtues, the whole value of gratitude lies in the spirit in which it is done; so, if this man's purpose be loyal, any shortcomings on his part are due not to himself, but to fortune. A man who is silent may, nevertheless, be eloquent; his hands may be folded or even bound, and he may yet be strong; just as a pilot is a pilot even when upon dry land, because his knowledge is complete, and there is nothing wanting to it, though there may be obstacles which prevent his making use of it. In the same way, a man is grateful who only wishes to be so, and who has no one but himself who can bear witness to his frame of mind. I will go even further than this: a man sometimes is grateful when he appears to be ungrateful, when ill-judging report has declared him to be so. Such a man can look to nothing but his own conscience, which can please him even when overwhelmed by calumny, which contradicts the mob and common rumour, relies only upon itself, and though it beholds a vast crowd of the other way of thinking opposed to it, does not count heads, but wins by its own vote alone. Should it see its own good faith meet with the punishment due to treachery, it will not descend from its pedestal, and will remain superior to its punishment. "I have," it says, "what I wished, what I strove for. I do not regret it, nor shall I do so; nor shall fortune, however unjust she may be, ever hear me say, 'What did I want? What now is the use of having meant well?'" A good conscience is of value on the rack, or in the fire; though fire be applied to each of our limbs, gradually encircle our living bodies, and burst our heart, yet if our heart be filled with a good conscience, it will rejoice in the fire which will make its good faith shine before the world.

XXII. Now let that question also which has been already stated be again brought forward; Why is it that we should wish to be grateful when we are dying, that we should carefully weigh the various services rendered us by different individuals, and carefully review our whole life, that we may not seem to have forgotten any kindness? Nothing then remains for us to hope for; yet when on the very threshold, we wish to depart from human life as full of gratitude as possible. There is in truth an immense reward for this thing merely in doing it, and what is honourable has great power to attract men's minds, which are overwhelmed by its beauty and carried off their balance, enchanted by its brilliancy and splendour. "Yet," argues our adversary, "from it many advantages take their rise, and good men obtain a safer life and love, and the good opinion of the better class, while their days are spent in greater security when accompanied by innocence and gratitude."

Indeed, nature would have been most unjust had she rendered this great blessing miserable, uncertain, and fruitless. But consider this point, whether you would make your way to that virtue, to which it is generally safe and easy to attain, even though the path lay over rocks and precipices, and were beset with fierce beasts and venomous serpents. A virtue is none the less to be desired for its own sake, because it has some adventitious profit connected with it: indeed, in most cases the noblest virtues are accompanied by many extraneous advantages, but it is the virtues that lead the way, and these merely follow in their train.

XXIII. Can we doubt that the climate of this abode of the

human race is regulated by the motion of the sun and moon in their orbits? that our bodies are sustained, the hard earth loosened, excessive moisture reduced, and the surly bonds of winter broken by the heat of the one, and that crops are brought to ripeness by the effectual all-pervading warmth of the other? that the fertility of the human race corresponds to the courses of the moon? that the sun by its revolution marks out the year, and that the moon, moving in a smaller orbit, marks out the months? Yet, setting aside all this, would not the sun be a sight worthy to be contemplated and worshipped, if he did no more than rise and set? would not the moon be worth looking at, even if it passed uselessly through the heavens? Whose attention is not arrested by the universe itself, when by night it pours forth its fires and glitters with innumerable stars? Who, while he admires them, thinks of their being of use to him? Look at that great company gliding over our heads, how they conceal their swift motion under the semblance of a fixed and immovable work. How much takes place in that night which you make use of merely to mark and count your days! What a mass of events is being prepared in that silence! What a chain of destiny their unerring path is forming! Those which you imagine to be merely strewn about for ornament are really one and all at work. Nor is there any ground for your belief that only seven stars revolve, and that the rest remain still: we understand the orbits of a few, but countless divinities, further removed from our sight, come and go; while the greater part of those whom our sight reaches move in a mysterious manner and by an unknown path.

XXIV. What then? would you not be captivated by the sight of such a stupendous work, even though it did not cover you, protect you, cherish you, bring you into existence and penetrate you with its spirit? Though these heavenly bodies are of the very first importance to us, and are, indeed, essential to our life, yet we can think of nothing but their glorious majesty, and similarly all virtue, especially that of gratitude, though it confers great advantages upon us, does not wish to be loved for that reason; it has something more in it than this, and he who merely reckons it among useful things does not perfectly comprehend it. A man, you say, is grateful because it is to his advantage to be so. If this be the case, then his advantage will be the measure of his gratitude. Virtue will not admit a covetous lover; men must approach her with open purse. The ungrateful man thinks, "I did wish to be grateful, but I fear the expense and danger and insults to which I should expose myself: I will rather consult my own interest." Men cannot be rendered grateful and ungrateful by the same line of reasoning: their actions are as distinct as their purposes. The one is ungrateful, although it is wrong, because it is his interest; the other is grateful, although it is not his interest, because it is right.

XXV. It is our aim to live in harmony with the scheme of the universe, and to follow the example of the gods. Yet in all their acts the gods have no object in view other than the act itself, unless you suppose that they obtain a reward for their work in the smoke of burnt sacrifices and the scent of incense. See what great things they do every day, how much they divide amongst us, with how great crops they fill the earth, how they move the seas with convenient winds to carry us to all shores, how by the fall of sudden showers they soften the ground, renew the dried-up springs of fountains, and call them into new life by unseen supplies of water. All this they do without reward, without any advantage accruing to themselves. Let our line of conduct, if it would not depart from its model, preserve this direction, and let us not act honourably because we are hired to do so. We ought to feel ashamed that any benefit should have a price: we pay nothing for the gods.

XXVI. "If," our adversary may say, "you wish to imitate the gods, then bestow benefits upon the ungrateful as well as the grateful; for the sun rises upon the wicked as well as the good, the seas are open even to pirates." By this question he really asks whether a good man would bestow a benefit upon an ungrateful person, knowing him to be ungrateful. Allow me here to introduce a short explanation, that we may not be taken in by a deceitful question. Understand that according to the system of the Stoics there are two classes of ungrateful persons. One man is ungrateful because he is a fool; a fool is a bad man; a man who is bad possesses every vice: therefore he is ungrateful. In the same way we speak of all bad men as dissolute, avaricious, luxurious, and spiteful, not because each man has all these vices in any great or remarkable degree, but because he might have them; they are in him, even though they be not seen. The second form of ungrateful person is he who is commonly meant by the term, one who is inclined by nature to this vice. In the case of him who has the vice of ingratitude just as he has every other, a wise man will bestow a benefit, because if he sets aside all such men there will be no one left for him to bestow it on. As for the ungrateful man who habitually misapplies benefits and acts so by choice, he will no more bestow a benefit upon him than he would lend money to a spendthrift, or place a deposit in the hands of one who had already often refused to many persons to give up the property with which they had entrusted him.

XXVII. We call some men timid because they are fools: in this they are like the bad men who are steeped in all vices without distinction. Strictly speaking, we call those persons timid who are alarmed even at unmeaning noises. A fool possesses all vices, but he is not equally inclined by nature to all; one is prone to avarice, another to luxury, and another to insolence. Those persons, therefore, are mistaken, who ask the Stoics, "What do you say, then? is Achilles timid? Aristides, who received a name for justice, is he unjust? Fabius, who 'by delays retrieved the day,' is he rash? Does Decius fear death? Is Mucius a traitor? Camillus a betrayer?" We do not mean that all vices are inherent in all men in the same way in which some especial ones are noticeable in certain men, but we declare that the bad man and the fool possess all vices; we do not even acquit them of fear when they are rash, or of avarice when they are extravagant. Just as a man has all his senses, yet all men have not on that account as keen a sight as Lynceus, so a man that is a fool has not all vices in so active and vigorous a form as some persons have spine of them, yet he has them all. All vices exist in all of them, yet all are not prominent in each individual. One man is naturally prone to avarice, another is the slave of wine, a third of lust; or, if not yet enslaved by these passions, he is so fashioned by nature that this is the direction in which his character would probably lead him. Therefore, to return to my original proposition, every bad man is ungrateful, because he has the seeds of every villainy in him; but he alone is rightly so called who is naturally inclined to this vice. Upon such a person as this, therefore, I shall not bestow a benefit. One who betrothed his daughter to an ill-tempered man from whom many women had sought a divorce, would be held to have neglected her interests; a man would be thought a bad father if he entrusted the care of his patrimony to one who had lost his own family estate, and it would be the act of a madman to make a will naming as the guardian of one's son a man who had already defrauded other wards. So will that man be said to bestow benefits as badly as possible, who chooses ungrateful persons, in whose hands they will perish.

XXVIII. "The gods," it may be said, "bestow much, even upon the ungrateful." But what they bestow they had prepared for the good, and the bad have their share as well, because they cannot be separated. It is better to benefit the bad as well, for the sake of benefiting the good, than to stint the good for fear of benefiting the bad. Therefore the gods have created all that you speak of, the day, the sun, the alternations of winter and summer, the transitions through spring and autumn from one extreme to the other, showers, drinking fountains, and regularly blowing winds for the use of all alike; they could not except individuals from the enjoyment of them. A king bestows honours upon those who deserve them, but he gives largesse to the undeserving as well. The thief, the bearer of false witness, and the adulterer, alike receive the public grant of corn, and all are placed on the register without any examination as to character; good and bad men share alike in all the other privileges which a man receives, because he is a citizen, not because he is a good man. God likewise has bestowed certain gifts upon the entire human race, from which no one is shut out. Indeed, it could not be arranged that the wind which was fair for good men should be foul for bad ones, while it is for the good of all men that the seas should be open for traffic and the kingdom of mankind be enlarged; nor could any law be appointed for the showers, so that they should not fall upon the fields of wicked and evil men. Some things are given to all alike: cities are founded for good and bad men alike; works of genius reach, by publication, even unworthy men; medicine points out the means of health even to the wicked; no one has checked the making up of wholesome remedies for fear that the undeserving should be healed. You must seek for examination and preference of individuals in such things as are bestowed separately upon those who are thought to deserve them; not in these, which admit the mob to share them without distinction. There is a great difference between not shutting a man out and choosing him. Even a thief receives justice; even murderers enjoy the blessings of peace; even those who have plundered others can recover their own property; assassins and private bravoes are defended against the common enemy by the city wall; the laws protect even those who have sinned most deeply against them. There are some things which no man could obtain unless they were given to all; you need not, therefore, cavil about those matters in which all mankind is invited to share. As for things which men receive or not at my discretion, I shall not bestow them upon one whom I know to be ungrateful.

XXIX. "Shall we, then," argues he, "not give our advice to an ungrateful man when he is at a loss, or refuse him a drink of water when he is thirsty, or not show him the path when he has lost his way? or would you do him these services and yet not give him anything?" Here I will draw a distinction, or at any rate endeavour to do so. A benefit is a useful service, yet all useful service is not a benefit; for some are so trifling as not to claim the title of benefits. To produce a benefit two conditions must concur. First, the importance of the thing given; for some things fall short of the dignity of a benefit. Who ever called a hunch of bread a benefit, or a farthing dole tossed to a beggar, or the means of lighting a fire? yet sometimes these are of more value than the most costly benefits; still their cheapness detracts from their value even when, by the exigency of time, they are rendered essential. The next condition, which is the most important of all, must necessarily be present, namely, that I should confer the benefit for the sake of him whom I wish to receive it, that I should judge him worthy of it, bestow it of my own free will, and receive pleasure from my own gift, none of which conditions are present in the cases of which we have just now spoken; for we do not bestow such things as those upon these who are worthy of them, but we give them carelessly, as trifles, and do not give them so much to a man as to humanity.

XXX. I shall not deny that sometimes I would give even to the unworthy, out of respect for others; as, for instance, in competition for public offices, some of the basest of men are preferred on account of their noble birth, to industrious men of no family, and that for good reasons; for the memory of great virtues is sacred, and more men will take pleasure in being good, if the respect felt for good men does not cease with their lives. What made Cicero's son a consul, except his father? What lately brought Cinna [Footnote: See Seneca on "Clemency," book i., ch.

ix.] out of the camp of the enemy and raised him to the consulate? What made Sextus Pompeius and the other Pompeii consuls, unless it was the greatness of one man, who once was raised so high that, by his very fall, he sufficiently exalted all his relatives. What lately made Fabius Persicus a member of more than one college of priests, though even profligates avoided his kiss? Was it not Verrucosus, and Allobrogicus, and the three hundred who to serve their country blocked the invader's path with the force of a single family? It is our duty to respect the virtuous, not only when present with us, but also when removed from our sight: as they have made it their study not to bestow their benefits upon one age alone, but to leave them existing after they themselves have passed away, so let us not confine our gratitude to a single age. If a man has begotten great men, he deserves to receive benefits, whatever he himself may be: he has given us worthy men. If a man descends from glorious ancestors, whatever he himself may be, let him find refuge under the shadow of his ancestry. As mean places are lighted up by the rays of the sun, so let the degenerate shine in the light of their forefathers.

XXXI. In this place, my Liberalis, I wish to speak in defence of the gods. We sometimes say, "What could Providence mean by placing an Arrhidaeus upon the throne?" Do you suppose that the crown was given to Arrhidaeus? nay, it was given to his father and his brother. Why did Heaven bestow the empire of the world upon Caius Caesar, the most bloodthirsty of mankind, who was wont to order blood to be shed in his presence as freely as if he wished to drink of it? Why, do you suppose that it was given to him? It was given to his father, Germanicus, to his grandfather, his great grandfather, and to others before them, no less illustrious men, though they lived as private citizens on a footing of equality with others. Why, when you yourself were making Mamercus Scaurus consul, were you ignorant of his vices? did he himself conceal them? did he wish to appear decent?

Did you admit a man who was so openly filthy to the fasces and the tribunal? Yes, it was because you were thinking of the great old Scaurus, the chief of the Senate, and were unwilling that his descendant should be despised.

XXXII. It is probable that the gods act in the same manner, that they show greater indulgence to some for the sake of their parents and their ancestry, and to others for the sake of their children and grandchildren, and a long line of descendants beyond them; for they know the whole course of their works, and have constant access to the knowledge of all that shall hereafter pass through their hands. These things come upon us from the unknown future, and the gods have foreseen and are familiar with the events by which we are startled. "Let these men," says Providence, "be kings, because their ancestors were good kings, because they regarded righteousness and temperance as the highest rule of life, because they did not devote the state to themselves, but devoted themselves to the state. Let these others reign, because some one of their ancestors before them was a good man, who bore a soul superior to fortune, who preferred to be conquered rather than to conquer in civil strife, because it was more to the advantage of the state. [Footnote: Gertz, "Stud. Crit," p. 159, note.] It was not possible to make a sufficient return to him for this during so long a time; let this other, therefore, out of regard for him, be chief of the people, not because he knows how, or is capable, but because the other has earned it for him. This man is misshapen, loathsome to look upon, and will disgrace the insignia of his office. Men will presently blame me, calling me blind and reckless, not knowing upon whom I am conferring what ought to be given to the greatest and noblest of men; but I know that, in giving this dignity to one man, I am paying an old debt to another. How should the men of today know that ancient hero, who so resolutely avoided the glory which pressed upon him, who went into danger with the same look which other men wear when they have escaped from danger, who never regarded his own interest as apart from that of the commonwealth?" "Where," you ask, "or who is he? whence does he come?" "You know him not; it lies with me to balance the debit and credit account in such cases as these; I know how much I owe to each man; I repay some after a long interval, others beforehand, according as my opportunities and the exigencies of my social system permit." I shall, therefore, sometimes bestow somewhat upon an ungrateful man, though not for his own sake.

XXXIII. "What," argues he, "if you do not know whether your man be ungrateful or grateful—will you wait until you know, or will you not lose the opportunity of bestowing a benefit? To wait is a long business—for, as Plato says, it is hard to form an opinion about the human mind,—not to wait, is rash." To this objector we shall answer, that we never should wait for absolute knowledge of the whole case, since the discovery of truth is an arduous task, but should proceed in the direction in which truth appeared to direct us. All our actions proceed in this direction: it is thus that we sow seed, that we sail upon the sea, that we serve in the army, marry, and bring up children. The result of all these actions is uncertain, so we take that course from which we believe that good results may be hoped for. Who can guarantee a harvest to the sower, a harbour to the sailor, victory to the soldier, a modest wife to the husband, dutiful children to the father? We proceed in the way in which reason, not absolute truth, directs us. Wait, do nothing that will not turn out well, form no opinion until you have searched but the truth, and your life will pass in absolute in action. Since it is only the appearance of truth, not truth itself, which leads me hither or thither, I shall confer benefits upon the man who apparently will be grateful.

XXXIV. "Many circumstances," argues he, "may arise which may enable a bad man to steal into the place of a good one, or may cause a good man to be disliked as though he were a bad one; for appearances, to which we trust, are deceptive." Who denies it? Yet I can find nothing else by which to guide my opinion. I must follow these tracks in my search after truth, for I have none more trustworthy than these; I will take pains to weigh the value of these with all possible care, and will not hastily give my assent to them. For instance, in a battle, it may happen that my hand may be deceived by some mistake into turning my weapon against my comrade, and sparing my enemy as though he were on my side; but this will not often take place, and will not take place through any fault of mine, for my object is to strike the enemy, and defend my countryman. If I know a man to be ungrateful, I shall not bestow a benefit upon him. But the man has passed himself off as a good man by some trick, and has imposed upon me. Well, this is not at all the fault of the giver, who gave under the impression that his friend was grateful. "Suppose," asks he, "that you were to promise to bestow a benefit, and afterwards were to learn that your man was ungrateful, would you bestow it or not? If you do, you do wrong knowingly, for you give to one to whom you ought not; if you refuse, you do wrong likewise, for you do not give to him to whom you promised to give. This case upsets your consistency, and that proud assurance of yours that the wise man never regrets his actions, or amends what he has done, or alters his plans." The wise man never changes his plans while the conditions under which he formed them remain the same; therefore, he never feels regret, because at the time nothing better than what he did could have been done, nor could any better decision have been arrived at than that which was made; yet he begins everything with the saving clause, "If nothing shall occur to the contrary." This is the reason why we say that all goes well with him, and that nothing happens contrary to his expectation, because he bears in mind the possibility of something happening to prevent the realization of his projects. It is an imprudent confidence to trust that fortune will be on our side. The wise man considers both sides: he knows how great is the power of errors, how uncertain human affairs are, how many obstacles there are to the success of plans. Without committing himself, he awaits the doubtful and capricious issue of events, and weighs certainty of purpose against uncertainty of result. Here also, however, he is protected by that saving clause, without which he decides upon nothing, and begins nothing.

XXXV. When I promise to bestow a benefit, I promise it, unless something occurs which makes it my duty not to do so. What if, for example, my country orders me to give to her what I had promised to my friend? or if a law be passed forbidding any one to do what I had promised to do for him? Suppose that I have promised you my daughter in marriage, that then you turn out to be a foreigner, and that I have no right of intermarriage with foreigners; in this case, the law, by which I am forbidden to fulfil my promise, forms my defence. I shall be treacherous, and hear myself blamed for inconsistency, only if I do not fulfil, my promise when all conditions remain the same as when I made it; otherwise, any change makes me free to reconsider the entire case, and absolves me from my promise. I may have promised to plead a cause; afterwards it appears that this cause is designed to form a precedent for an attack upon my father. I may have promised to leave my country, and travel abroad; then news comes that the road is beset with robbers. I was going to an appointment at some particular place; but my son's illness, or my wife's confinement, prevented me. All conditions must be the same as they were when I made the promise, if you mean to hold me bound in honour to fulfil it. Now what greater change can take place than that I should discover you to be a bad and ungrateful man? I shall refuse to an unworthy man that which I had intended to give him supposing him to be worthy, and I shall also have reason to be angry with him for the trick which he has put upon me.

XXXVI. I shall nevertheless look into the matter, and consider what the value of the thing promised may be. If it be trifling, I shall give it, not because you are worthy of it, but because I promised it, and I shall not give it as a present, but merely in order to make good my words and give myself a twitch of the ear. I will punish my own rashness in promising by the loss of what I gave. "See how grieved you are; mind you take more care what you say in future." As the saying is, I will take tongue money from you. If the matter be important, I will not, as Maecenas said, let ten million sesterces reproach me. I will weigh the two sides of the question one against the other: there is something in abiding by what you have promised; on the other hand, there is a great deal in not bestowing a benefit upon one who is unworthy of it. Now, how great is this benefit? If it is a trifling one, let us wink and let it pass; but if it will cause me much loss or much shame to give it, I had rather excuse myself once for refusing it than have to do so ever after for giving it. The whole point, I repeat, depends upon how much the thing given is worth: let the terms of my promise be appraised. Not only shall I refuse to give what I may have promised rashly, but I shall also demand back again what I may have wrongly bestowed: a man must be mad who keeps a promise made under a mistake.

XXXVII. Philip, king of the Macedonians, had a hardy soldier whose services he had found useful in many campaigns. From time to time he made this man presents of part of the plunder as the reward of his valour, and used to excite his greedy spirit by his frequent gifts. This man was cast by shipwreck upon the estate of a certain Macedonian, who as soon as he heard the news hastened to him, restored his breath, removed him to his own farmhouse, gave up his own bed to him, nursed him out of his weakened and half-dead condition, took care of him at his own expense for thirty days, restored him to health and gave him a sum of money for his journey, as the man kept constantly saying, "If only I can see my chief, I will repay your kindness." He told Philip of his shipwreck, said nothing about the help which he had received, and at once demanded that a certain man's estate should be given to him. The man was a friend of his: it was that very man by whom he had been rescued and restored to health. Sometimes, especially in time of war, kings bestow many gifts with their eyes shut. One just man cannot deal with such a mass of armed selfishness. It is not possible for any one to be at the same time a good man and a good general. How are so many thousands of insatiable men to be satiated? What would they have, if every man had his own? Thus Philip reasoned with himself while he ordered the man to be put in possession of the property which he asked for. However, the other, when driven out of his estate, did not, like a peasant, endure his wrongs in silence, thankful that he himself was not given away also, but sent a sharp and outspoken letter to Philip, who, on reading it, was so much enraged that he straightway ordered Pausanias to restore the property to its former owner, and to brand that wickedest of soldiers, that most ungrateful of guests, that greediest of shipwrecked men, with letters bearing witness to his ingratitude. He, indeed, deserved to have the letters not merely branded but carved in his flesh, for having reduced his host to the condition in which he himself had been when he lay naked and shipwrecked upon the beach; still, let us see within what limits one ought to keep in punishing him. Of course what he had so villainously seized ought to be taken from him. But who would be affected by the spectacle of his punishment? The crime which he had committed would prevent his being pitied even by any humane person.

XXXVIII. Will Philip then give you a thing because he has promised to give it, even though he ought not to do so, even though he will commit a wrong by doing so, nay, a crime, even though by this one act he will make it impossible for shipwrecked men to reach the shore? There is no inconsistency in giving up an intention which we have discovered to be wrong and have condemned as wrong; we ought candidly to admit, "I thought that it was something different; I have been deceived." It is mere pride and folly to persist, "what I once have said, be it what it may, shall remain unaltered and settled." There is no disgrace in altering one's plans according to circumstances. Now, if Philip had left this man in possession of that seashore which he obtained by his shipwreck, would he not have practically pronounced sentence of banishment against all unfortunates for the future? "Rather," says Philip, "do thou carry upon thy forehead of brass those letters, that they may be impressed upon the eyes of all throughout my kingdom. Go, let men see how sacred a thing is the table of hospitality; show them your face, that upon it they may read the decree which prevents its being a capital crime to give refuge to the unfortunate under one's roof. The order will be more certainly respected by this means than if I had inscribed it upon tablets of brass."

XXXIX. "Why then," argues our adversary, "did your Stoic philosopher Zeno, when he had promised a loan of five hundred denarii to some person, whom he afterwards discovered to be of doubtful character, persist in lending it, because of his promise, though his friends dissuaded him from doing so?" In the first place a loan is on a different footing to a benefit. Even when we have lent money to an undesirable person we can recall it; I can demand payment upon a certain day, and if he becomes bankrupt, I can obtain my share of his property; but a benefit is lost utterly and instantly. Besides, the one is the act of a bad man, the other that of a bad father of a family. In the next place, if the sum had been a larger one, not even Zeno would have persisted in lending it. It was five hundred denarii; the sort of sum of which one says, "May he spend it in sickness," and it was worth paying so much to avoid breaking his promise. I shall go out to supper, even though the weather be cold, because I have promised to go; but I shall not if snow be falling. I shall leave my bed to go to a betrothal feast, although I may be suffering from indigestion; but I shall not do so if I am feverish. I will become bail for you, because I promised; but not if you wish me to become bail in some transaction of uncertain issue, if you expose me to forfeiting my money to the state. There runs through all these cases, I argue, an implied exception; if I am able, provided it is right for me to do so, if these things be so and so. Make the position the same when you ask me to fulfil my promise, as it was when I gave it, and it will be mere fickleness to disappoint you; but if something new has taken place in the meanwhile, why should you wonder at my intentions being changed when the conditions under which I gave the promise are changed? Put everything back as it was, and I shall be the same as I was. We enter into recognizances to appear, yet if we fail to do so an action will not in all cases lie against us, for we are excused for making default if forced to do so by a power which we cannot resist.

XL. You may take the same answer to the question as to whether we ought in all cases to show gratitude for kindness, and whether a benefit ought in all cases to be repaid. It is my duty to show a grateful mind, but in some cases my own poverty, in others the prosperity of the friend to whom I owe some return, will not permit me to give it. What, for instance, am I, a poor man, to give to a king or a rich man in return for his kindness, especially as some men regard it as a wrong to have their benefits repaid, and are wont to pile one benefit upon another? In dealing with such persons, what more can I do than wish to repay them? Yet I ought not to refuse to receive a new benefit, because I have not repaid the former one. I shall take it as freely as it is given, and will offer myself to my friend as a wide field for the exercise of his good nature: he who is unwilling to receive new benefits must be dissatisfied with what he has already received. Do you say, "I shall not be able to return them?" What is that to the purpose? I am willing enough to do so if opportunity or means were given me. He gave it to me, of course, having both opportunity and means: is he a good man or a bad one? if he is a good man, I have a good case against him, and I will not plead if he be a bad one. Neither do I think it right to insist on making repayment, even though it be against the will of those whom we repay, and to press it upon them however reluctant they may be; it is not repayment to force an unwilling man to resume what you were once willing to take. Some people, if any trifling present be sent to them, afterwards send back something else for no particular reason, and then declare that they are under no obligation; to send something back at once, and balance one present by another, is the next thing to refusing to receive it. On some occasions I shall not return a benefit, even though I be able to do so. When? When by so doing I shall myself lose more than he will gain, or if he would not notice any advantage to himself in receiving that which it would be a great loss to me to return. The man who is always eager to repay under all circumstances, has not the feeling of a grateful man, but of a debtor; and, to put it shortly, he who is too eager to repay, is unwilling to be in his friend's debt; he who is unwilling, and yet is in his friend's debt, is ungrateful.

BOOK V.

I.

In the preceding books I seem to have accomplished the object which I proposed to myself, since in them I have discussed how a benefit ought to be bestowed, and how it ought to be received. These are the limits of this action; when I dwell upon it further I am not obeying the orders, but the caprices of my subject which ought to be followed whither it leads, not whither it allures us to wander; for now and then something will arise, which, although it is all but unconnected with the subject, instead of being a necessary part of it, still thrills the mind with a certain charm. However, since you wish it to be so, let us go on, after having completed our discussion of the heads of the subject itself, to investigate those matters which, if you wish for truth, I must call adjacent to it, not actually connected with it; to examine which carefully is not one worth one's while, and yet is not labour in vain. No praise, however, which I can give to benefits does justice to you, Aebutius Liberalis, a man of excellent disposition and naturally inclined to bestow them. Never have I seen any one esteem even the most trifling services more kindly; indeed, your good-nature goes so far as to regard whatever benefit is bestowed upon anyone as bestowed upon yourself; you are prepared to pay even what is owed by the ungrateful, that no one may regret having bestowed benefits. You yourself are so far from any boastfulness, you are so eager at once to free those whom you serve from any feeling of obligation to you, that you like, when giving anything to any one, to seem not so much to be giving a present as returning one; and therefore what you give in this manner will all the more fully he repaid to you: for, as a rule, benefits come to one who does not demand repayment of them; and just as glory follows those who avoid it, so men receive a more plentiful harvest in return for benefits bestowed upon those who had it in their power to be ungrateful. With you there is no reason why those who have received benefits from you should not ask for fresh ones; nor would you refuse to bestow others, to overlook and conceal what you have given, and to add to it more and greater gifts, since it is the aim of all the best men and the noblest dispositions to bear with an ungrateful man until you make him grateful. Be not deceived in pursuing this plan; vice, if you do not too soon begin to hate it, will yield to virtue.

II. Thus it is that you are especially pleased with what you think the grandly-sounding phrase, "It is disgraceful to be worsted in a contest of benefits." Whether this be true or not deserves to be investigated, and it means something quite different from what you imagine; for it is never disgraceful to be worsted in any honourable contest, provided that you do not throw down your arms, and that even when conquered you wish to conquer. All men do not strive for a good object with the same strength, resources, and good fortune, upon which depend at all events the issues of the most admirable projects, though we ought to praise the will itself which makes an effort in the right direction. Even though another passes it by with swifter pace, yet the palm of victory does not, as in publicly-exhibited races, declare which is the better man; though even in the games chance frequently brings an inferior man to the front. As far as loyalty of feeling goes, which each man wishes to be possessed in the fullest measure on his own side, if one of the two be the more powerful, if he have at his disposal all the resources which he wishes to use, and be favoured by fortune in his most ambitious efforts, while the other, although equally willing, can only return less than he receives, or perhaps can make no return at all, but still wishes to do so and is entirely devoted to this object; then the latter is no more conquered than he who dies in arms, whom the enemy found it easier to slay than to turn back. To be conquered, which you consider disgraceful, cannot happen to a good man; for he will never surrender, never give up the contest, to the last day of his life he will stand prepared and in that posture he will die, testifying that though he has received much, yet that he had the will to repay as much as he had received.

III. The Lacedaemonians forbid their young men to contend in the pancratium, or with the caestus, in which games the defeated party has to acknowledge himself beaten. The winner of a race is he who first reaches the goal; he outstrips the others in swiftness, but not in courage. The wrestler who has been thrown three times loses the palm of victory, but does not yield it up. Since the Lacedaemonians thought it of great importance that their countrymen should be invincible, they kept them away from those contests in which victory is assigned, not by the judge, or by the issue of the contest itself, but by the voice of the vanquished begging the victor to spare him as he falls. This attribute of never being conquered, which they so jealously guard among their citizens, can be attained by all men through virtue and goodwill, because even when all else is vanquished, the mind remains unconquered. For this cause no one speaks of the three hundred Fabii as conquered, but slaughtered. Regulus was taken captive by the Carthaginians, not conquered; and so were all other men who have not yielded in spirit when overwhelmed by the strength and weight of angry fortune.

So is it with benefits. A man may have received more than he gave, more valuable ones, more frequently bestowed; yet is he not vanquished. It may be that, if you compare the benefits with one another, those which he has received will outweigh those which he has bestowed; but if you compare the giver and the receiver, whose intentions also ought to be considered apart, neither will prove the victor. It often happens that even when one combatant is pierced with many wounds, while the other is only slightly injured, yet they are said to have fought a drawn battle, although the former may appear to be the worse man.

IV. No one, therefore, can be conquered in a contest of benefits, if he knows how to owe a debt, if he wishes to make a return for what he has received, and raises himself to the same level with his friend in spirit, though he cannot do so in material gifts. As long as he remains in this temper of mind, as long as he has the wish to declare by proofs that he has a grateful mind, what difference does it make upon which side we can count the greater number of presents? You are able to give much; I can do nothing but receive. Fortune abides with you, goodwill alone with me; yet I am as much on an equality with you as naked or lightly armed men are with a large body armed to the teeth.

No one, therefore, is worsted by benefits, because each man's gratitude is to be measured by his will. If it be disgraceful to be worsted in a contest of benefits, you ought not to receive a benefit from very powerful men whose kindness you cannot return, I mean such as princes and kings, whom fortune has placed in such a station that they can give away much, and can only receive very little and quite inadequate returns for what they give. I have spoken of kings and princes, who alone can cause works to be accomplished, and whose superlative power depends upon the obedience and services of inferiors; but some there are, free from all earthly lusts, who are scarcely affected by any human objects of desire, upon whom fortune herself could bestow nothing. I must be worsted in a contest of benefits with Socrates, or with Diogenes, who walked naked through the treasures of Macedonia, treading the king's wealth under his feet. In good sooth, he must then rightly have seemed, both to himself and to all others whose eyes were keen enough to perceive the real truth, to be superior even to him at whose feet all the world lay. He was far more powerful, far richer even than Alexander, who then possessed everything; for there was more that Diogenes could refuse to receive than that Alexander was able to give.

V. It is not disgraceful to be worsted by these men, for I am not the less brave because you pit me against an invulnerable enemy, nor does fire not burn because you throw into it something over which flames have no power, nor does iron lose its power of cutting, though you may wish to cut up a stone which is hard, impervious to blows, and of such a nature that hard tools are blunted upon it. I give you the same answer about gratitude. A man is not disgracefully worsted in a contest of benefits if he lays himself under an obligation to such persons as these, whose enormous wealth or admirable virtue shut out all possibility of their benefits being returned. As a rule we are worsted by our parents; for while we have them with us, we regard them as severe, and do not understand what they do for us. When our age begins to bring us a little sense, and we gradually perceive that they deserve our love for those very things which used to prevent our loving them, their advice, their punishments, and the careful watch which they used to keep over our youthful recklessness, they are taken from us. Few live to reap any real fruit from children; most men feel their sons only as a burden. Yet there is no disgrace in being worsted by one's parent in bestowing benefits; how should there be, seeing that there is no disgrace in being worsted by anyone. We are equal to some men, and yet not equal; equal in intention, which is all that they care for, which is all that we promise to be, but unequal in fortune. And if fortune prevents any one from repaying a kindness, he need not, therefore, blush, as though he were vanquished; there is no disgrace in failing to reach your object, provided you attempt to reach it. It often is necessary, that before making any return for the benefits which we have received, we should ask for new ones; yet, if so, we shall not refrain from asking for them, nor shall we do so as though disgraced by so doing, because, even if we do not repay the debt, we shall owe it; because, even if something from without befalls us to prevent our repaying it, it will not be our fault if we are not grateful. We can neither be conquered in intention, nor can we be disgraced by yielding to what is beyond our strength to contend with.

VI. Alexander, the king of the Macedonians, used to boast that he had never been worsted by anybody in a contest of benefits. If so, it was no reason why, in the fulness of his pride, he should despise the Macedonians, Greeks, Carians, Persians, and other tribes of whom his army was composed, nor need he imagine that it was this that gave him an empire reaching from a corner of Thrace to the shore of the unknown sea. Socrates could make the same boast, and so could Diogenes, by whom Alexander was certainly surpassed; for was he not surpassed on the day when, swelling as he was beyond the limits of merely human pride, he beheld one to whom he could give nothing, from whom he could take nothing? King Archelaus invited Socrates to come to him. Socrates is reported to have answered that he should be sorry to go to one who would bestow benefits upon him, since he should not be able to make him an adequate return for them. In the first place, Socrates was at liberty not to receive them; next, Socrates himself would have been the first to bestow a benefit, for he would have come when invited, and would have given to Archelaus that for which Archelaus could have made no return to Socrates. Even if Archelaus were to give Socrates gold and silver, if he learned in return for them to despise gold and silver, would not Socrates be able to repay Archelaus? Could Socrates receive from him as much value as he gave, in displaying to him a man skilled in the knowledge of life and of death, comprehending the true purpose of each? Suppose that he had found this king, as it were, groping his way in the clear sunlight, and had taught him the secrets of nature, of which he was so ignorant, that when there was an eclipse of the sun, he up his palace, and shaved his son's head, [Footnote: Gertz very reasonably conjectures that he shaved his own head which reading would require a very trifling alteration of the text.] which men are wont to do in times of mourning and distress. What a benefit it would have been if he had dragged the terror-stricken king out of his hiding-place, and bidden him be of good cheer, saying, "This is not a disappearance of the sun, but a conjunction of two heavenly bodies; for the moon, which proceeds along a lower path, has placed her disk beneath the sun, and hidden it by the interposition of her own mass. Sometimes she only hides a small portion of the sun's disk, because she only grazes it in passing; sometimes she hides more, by placing more of herself before it; and sometimes she shuts it out from our sight altogether, if she passes in an exactly even course between the sun and the earth. Soon, however, their own swift motion will draw these two bodies apart; soon the earth will receive back again the light of day. And this system will continue throughout centuries, having certain days, known beforehand, upon which the sun cannot display all rays, because of the intervention of the moon. Wait only for a short time; he will soon emerge, he will soon leave that seeming cloud, and freely shed abroad his light without any hindrances." Could Socrates not have made an adequate return to Archelaus, if he had taught him to reign? as though Socrates would not benefit him sufficiently, merely by enabling him to bestow a benefit upon Socrates. Why, then, did Socrates say this? Being a joker and a speaker in parables—a man who turned all, especially the great, into ridicule—he preferred giving him a satirical refusal, rather than an obstinate or haughty one, and therefore said that he did not wish to receive benefits from one to whom he could not return as much as he received. He feared, perhaps, that he might be forced to receive something which he did not wish, he feared that it might be something unfit for Socrates to receive. Some one may say, "He ought to have said that he did not wish to go." But by so doing he would have excited against himself the anger of an arrogant king, who wished everything connected with himself to be highly valued. It makes no difference to a king whether you be unwilling to give anything to him or to accept anything from him; he is equally incensed at either rebuff, and to be treated with disdain is more bitter to a proud spirit than not to be feared. Do you wish to know what Socrates really meant? He, whose freedom of speech could not be borne even by a free state, was not willing of his own choice to become a slave.

VII. I think that we have sufficiently discussed this part of the subject, whether it be disgraceful to be worsted in a contest of benefits. Whoever asks this question must know that men are not wont to bestow benefits upon themselves, for evidently it could not be disgraceful to be worsted by oneself. Yet some of the Stoics debate this question, whether any one can confer a benefit upon himself, and whether one ought to return one's own kindness to oneself. This discussion has been raised in consequence of our habit of saying, "I am thankful to myself," "I can complain of no one but myself," "I am angry with myself," "I will punish myself," "I hate myself," and many other phrases of the same sort, in which one speaks of oneself as one would of some other person. "If," they argue, "I can injure myself, why should I not be able also to bestow a benefit upon myself? Besides this, why are those things not called benefits when I bestow them upon myself which would be called benefits if I bestowed them upon another? If to receive a certain thing from another would lay me under an obligation to him, how is it that if I give it to myself, I do not contract an obligation to myself? why should I be ungrateful to my own self, which is no less disgraceful than it is to be mean to oneself, or hard and cruel to oneself, or neglectful of oneself?" The procurer is equally odious whether he prostitutes others or himself. We blame a flatterer, and one who imitates another man's mode of speech, or is prepared to give praise whether it be deserved or not; we ought equally to blame one who humours himself and looks up to himself, and so to speak is his own flatterer. Vices are not only hateful when outwardly practised, but also when they are repressed within the mind. Whom would you admire more than he who governs himself and has himself under command? It is easier to rule savage nations, impatient of foreign control, than to restrain one's own mind and keep it under one's own control. Plato, it is argued, was grateful to Socrates for having been taught by him;

why should not Socrates be grateful to himself for having taught himself? Marcus Cato said, "Borrow from yourself whatever you lack;" why, then, if I can lend myself anything, should I be unable to give myself anything? The instances in which usage divides us into two persons are innumerable; we are wont to say, "Let me converse with myself," and, "I will give myself a twitch of the ear;" [Footnote: See book iv. ch. xxxvi.] and if it be true that one can do so, then a man ought to be grateful to himself, just as he is angry with himself; as he blames himself, SO he ought to praise himself; since he can impoverish himself, he can also enrich himself. Injuries and benefits are the converse of one another: if we say of a man, 'he has done himself an injury,' we can also say 'he has bestowed upon himself a benefit?'

VIII. It is natural that a man should first incur an obligation, and then that he should return gratitude for it; a debtor cannot exist without a creditor, any more than a husband without a wife, or a son without a father; someone must give in order that some one may receive. Just as no one carries himself, although he moves his body and transports it from place to place; as no one, though he may have made a speech in his own defence, is said to have stood by himself, or erects a statue to himself as his own patron; as no sick man, when by his own care he has regained his health, asks himself for a fee; so in no transaction, even when a man does what is useful to himself, need he return thanks to himself, because there is no one to whom he can return them. Though I grant that a man can bestow a benefit upon himself, yet at the same time that he gives it, he also receives it; though I grant that a man may receive a benefit from himself, yet he receives it at the same time that he gives it. The exchange takes place within doors, as they say, and the transfer is made at once, as though the debt were a fictitious one; for he who gives is not a different person to he who receives, but one and the same. The word "to owe" has no meaning except as between two persons; how then can it apply to one man who incurs an obligation, and by the same act frees himself from it? In a disk or a ball there is no top or bottom, no beginning or end, because the relation of the parts is changed when it moves, what was behind coming before, and what went down on one side coming up on the other, so that all the parts, in whatever direction they may move, come back to the same position. Imagine that the same thing takes place in a man; into however many pieces you may divide him, he remains one. If he strikes himself, he has no one to call to account for the insult; if he binds himself and locks himself up, he cannot demand damages; if he bestows a benefit upon himself, he straightway returns it to the giver. It is said that there is no waste in nature, because everything which is taken from nature returns to her again, and nothing can perish, because it cannot fall out of nature, but goes round again to the point from whence it started. You ask, "What connection has this illustration with the subject?" I will tell you. Imagine yourself to be ungrateful, the benefit bestowed upon you is not lost, he who gave it has it; suppose that you are unwilling to receive it, it still belongs to you before it is returned. You cannot lose anything, because what you take away from yourself, you nevertheless gain yourself. The matter revolves in a circle within yourself; by receiving you give, by giving you receive.

IX. "It is our duty," argues our adversary, "to bestow benefits upon ourselves, therefore we ought also to be grateful to ourselves." The original axiom, upon which the inference depends, is untrue, for no one bestows benefits upon himself, but obeys the dictates of his nature, which disposes him to affection for himself, and which makes him take the greatest pains to avoid hurtful things, and to follow after those things which are profitable to him. Consequently, the man who gives to himself is not generous, nor is he who pardons himself forgiving, nor is he who is touched by his own misfortunes tender-hearted; it is natural to do those things to oneself which when done to others become generosity, clemency, and tenderness of heart. A benefit is a voluntary act, but to do good to oneself is an instinctive one. The more benefits a man bestows, the more beneficent he is, yet who ever was praised for having been of service to himself? or for having rescued himself from brigands? No one bestows a benefit upon himself any more than he bestows hospitality upon himself; no one gives himself anything, any more than he lends himself anything. If each man bestows benefits upon himself, is always bestowing them, and bestows them without any cessation, then it is impossible for him to make any calculation of the number of his benefits; when then can he show his gratitude, seeing that by the very act of doing so he would bestow a benefit? for what distinction can you draw between giving himself a benefit or receiving a benefit for himself, when the whole transaction takes place in the mind of the same man? Suppose that I have freed myself from danger, then I have bestowed a benefit upon myself; suppose I free myself a second time, by so doing do I bestow or repay a benefit? In the next place, even if I grant the primary axiom, that we can bestow benefits upon ourselves, I do not admit that which follows; for even if we can do so, we ought not to do so. Wherefore? Because we receive a return for them at once. It is right for me to receive a benefit, then to lie under an obligation, then to repay it; now here there is no time for remaining under an obligation, because we receive the return without any delay. No one really gives except to another, no one owes except to another, no one repays except to another. An act which always requires two persons cannot take place within the mind of one.

X. A benefit means the affording of something useful, and the word AFFORDING implies other persons. Would not a man be thought mad if he said that he had sold something to himself, because selling means alienation, and the transferring of a thing and of one's rights in that thing to another person? Yet giving, like selling anything, consists in making it pass away from you, handing over what you yourself once owned into the keeping of some one else.

If this be so, no one ever gave himself a benefit, because no one gives to himself; if not, two opposites coalesce, so that it becomes the same thing to give and to receive. Yet there is a great difference between giving and receiving; how should there not be, seeing that these words are the converse of one another? Still, if any one can give himself a benefit, there can be no difference between giving and receiving. I said a little before that some words apply only to other persons, and are so constituted that their whole meaning lies apart from ourselves; for instance, I am a brother, but a brother of some other man, for no one is his own brother; I am an equal, but equal to somebody else, for who is equal to himself? A thing which is compared to another thing is unintelligible without that other thing; a thing which is joined to something else does not exist apart from it; so that which is given does not exist without the other person, nor can a benefit have any existence without another person. This is clear from the very phrase which describes it, 'to do good,' yet no one does good to himself, any more than he favours himself or is on his own side. I might enlarge further upon this subject and give many examples. Why should benefits not be included among those acts which require two persons to perform them? Many honourable, most admirable and highly virtuous acts cannot take place without a second person. Fidelity is praised and held to be one of the chief blessings known among men, yet was any one ever on that account said to have kept faith with himself?

XI. I come now to the last part of this subject. The man who returns a kindness ought to expend something, just as he who repays expends money; but the man who returns a kindness to himself expends nothing, just as he who receives a benefit from himself gains nothing. A benefit and gratitude for it must pass to and fro between two persons; their interchange cannot take place within one man. He who returns a kindness does good in his turn to him from whom he has received something; but the man who returns his own kindness, to whom does he do good? To himself? Is there any one who does not regard the returning of a kindness, and the bestowal of a benefit, as distinct acts? 'He who returns a kindness to himself does good to himself.' Was any man ever unwilling to do this, even though he were ungrateful? nay, who ever was ungrateful from any other motive than this? "If," it is argued, "we are right in thanking ourselves, we ought to return our own kindness;" yet we say, "I am thankful to myself for having refused to marry that woman," or "for having refused to join a partnership with that man." When we speak thus, we are really praising ourselves, and make use of the language of those who return thanks to approve our own acts. A benefit is something which, when given, may or may not be returned. Now, he who gives a benefit to himself must needs receive what he gives; therefore, this is not a benefit. A benefit is received at one time, and is returned at another; (but when a man bestows a benefit upon himself, he both receives it and returns it at the same time). In a benefit, too, what we commend and admire is, that a man has for the time being forgotten his own interests, in order that he may do good to another; that he has deprived himself of something, in order to bestow it upon another. Now, he who bestows a benefit upon himself does not do this. The bestowal of a benefit is an act of companionship—it wins some man's friendship, and lays some man under an obligation; but to bestow it upon oneself is no act of companionship—it wins no man's friendship, lays no man under an obligation, raises no man's hopes, or leads him to say, "This man must be courted; he bestowed a benefit upon that person, perhaps he will bestow one upon me also." A benefit is a thing which one gives not for one's own sake, but for the sake of him to whom it is given; but he who bestows a benefit upon himself, does so for his own sake; therefore, it is not a benefit.

XII. Now I seem to you not to have made good what I said at the beginning of this book. You say that I am far from doing what is worth any one's while; nay, that in real fact I have thrown away all my trouble. Wait, and soon you will be able to say this more truly, for I shall lead you into covert lurking-places, from which when you have escaped, you will have gained nothing except that you will have freed yourself from difficulties with which you need never have hampered yourself. What is the use of laboriously untying knots which you yourself have tied, in order that you might untie them? Yet, just as some knots are tied in fun and for amusement, so that a tyro may find difficulty in untying them, which knots he who tied them can loose without any trouble, because he knows the joinings and the difficulties of them, and these nevertheless afford us some pleasure, because they test the sharpness of our wits, and engross, our attention; so also these questions, which seem subtle and tricky, prevent our intellects becoming careless and lazy, for they ought at one time to have a field given them to level, in order that they may wander about it, and at another to have some dark and rough passage thrown in their way for them to creep through, and make their way with caution. It is said by our opponent that no one is ungrateful; and this is supported by the following arguments: "A benefit is that which does good; but, as you Stoics say, no one can do good to a bad man; therefore, a bad man does not receive a benefit. (If he does not receive it, he need not return it; therefore, no bad man is ungrateful.) Furthermore, a benefit is an honourable and commendable thing. No honourable or commendable thing can find any place with a bad man; therefore, neither can a benefit. If he cannot receive one, he need not repay one; therefore, he does not become ungrateful. Moreover, as you say, a good man does everything rightly; if he does everything rightly, he cannot be ungrateful. A good man returns a benefit, a bad man does not receive one. If this be so, no man, good or bad, can be ungrateful. Therefore, there is no such thing in nature as an ungrateful man: the word is meaningless." We Stoics have only one kind of good, that which is honourable. This cannot come to a bad man, for he would cease to be bad if virtue entered into him; but as long as he is bad, no one can bestow a benefit upon him, because good and bad are contraries, and cannot exist together. Therefore, no one can do good to such a man, because whatever he receives is corrupted by his vicious way of using it. Just as the stomach, when disordered by disease and secreting bile, changes all the food which it receives, and turns every kind of sustenance into a source of pain, so whatever you entrust to an ill-regulated mind becomes to it a burden, an annoyance, and a source of misery. Thus the most prosperous and the richest men have the most trouble; and the more property they have to perplex them, the less likely they are to find out what they really are. Nothing, therefore, can reach bad men which would do them good; nay, nothing which would not do them harm. They change whatever falls to their lot into their own evil nature; and things which elsewhere would, if given to better men, be both beautiful and profitable, are ruinous to them. They cannot, therefore, bestow benefits, because no one can give what he does not possess, and, therefore, they lack the pleasure of doing good to others.

XIII. But, though this be so, yet even a bad man can receive some things which resemble benefits, and he will be ungrateful if he does not return them. There are good things belonging to the mind, to the body, and to fortune. A fool or a bad man is debarred from the first—those, that is, of the mind; but he is admitted to a share in the two latter, and, if he does not return them, he is ungrateful. Nor does this follow from our (Stoic) system alone the Peripatetics, also, who widely extend the boundaries of human happiness, declare that trifling benefits reach bad men, and that he who does not return them is ungrateful. We therefore do not agree that things which do not tend to improve the mind should be called benefits, yet do not deny that these things are convenient and desirable. Such things as these a bad man may bestow upon a good man, or may receive from him—such, for example, as money, clothes, public office, or life; and, if he makes no return for these, he will come under the denomination of ungrateful. "But how can you call a man ungrateful for not returning that which you say is not a benefit?" Some things, on account of their similarity, are included under the same designation, although they do not really deserve it. Thus we speak of a silver or golden box; ["The original word is 'pyx,' which means a box made of box-wood."] thus we call a man illiterate, although he may not be utterly ignorant, but only not acquainted with the higher branches of literature; thus, seeing a badly-dressed ragged man we say that we have seen a naked man. These things of which we spoke are not benefits, but they possess the appearance of benefits. "Then, just as they are quasi-benefits, so your man is quasi-ungrateful, not really ungrateful." This is untrue, because both he who gives and he who receives them speaks of them as benefits; so he who fails to return the semblance of a real benefit is as much an ungrateful man as he who mixes a sleeping draught, believing it to be poison, is a poisoner.

XIV. Cleanthes speaks more impetuously than this. "Granted," says he, "that what he received was not a benefit, yet he is ungrateful, because he would not have returned a benefit if he had received one." So he who carries deadly weapons and has intentions of robbing and murdering, is a brigand even before he has dipped his hands in blood; his wickedness consists and is shown in action, but does not begin thereby. Men are punished for sacrilege, although no one's hands can reach to the gods. "How," asks our opponent, "can any one be ungrateful to a bad man, since a bad man cannot bestow a benefit?" In the same way, I answer, because that which he received was not a benefit, but was called one; if any one receives from a bad man any of those things which are valued by the ignorant, and of which bad men often possess great store, it becomes his duty to make a return in the same kind, and to give back as though they were truly good those things which he received as though they were truly good. A man is said to be in debt, whether he owes gold pieces or leather marked with a state stamp, such as the Lacedaemonians used, which passes for coined money. Pay your debts in that kind in which you incurred them. You have nothing to do with the definition of benefits, or with the question whether so great and noble a name ought to be degraded by applying it to such vulgar and mean matters as these, nor do we seek for truth that we may use it to the disadvantage of others; do you adjust your minds to the semblance of truth, and while you are learning what is really honourable, respect everything to which the name of honour is applied.

XV. "In the same way," argues our adversary, "that your school proves that no one is ungrateful, you afterwards prove that all men are ungrateful. For, as you say, all fools are bad men; he who has one vice has all vices; all men are both fools and bad men; therefore all men are ungrateful." Well, what then? Are they not? Is not this the universal reproach of the human race? is there not a general complaint that benefits are thrown away, and that there are very few men who do not requite their benefactors with the basest ingratitude? Nor need you suppose that what we say is merely the grumbling of men who think every act wicked and depraved which falls short of an ideal standard of righteousness. Listen! I know not who it is who speaks, yet the voice with which he condemns mankind proceeds, not from the schools of philosophers, but from the midst of the crowd:

"Host is not safe from guest;
Father-in-law from son; but seldom love
Exists 'twixt brothers; wives long to destroy
Their husbands; husbands long to slay their wives."

This goes even further: according to this, crimes take the place of benefits, and men do not shrink from shedding the blood of those for whom they ought to shed their own; we requite benefits by steel and poison. We call laying violent hands upon our own country, and putting down its resistance by the fasces of its own lictors, gaining power and great place; every man thinks himself to be in a mean and degraded position if he has not raised himself above the constitution; the armies which are received from the state are turned against her, and a general now says to his men, "Fight against your wives, fight against your children, march in arms against your altars, your hearths and homes!" Yes, [Footnote: I believe, in spite of Gertz, that this is part of the speech of the Roman general, and that the conjecture of Muretus, "without the command of the senate," gives better sense.] you, who even when about to triumph ought not to enter the city at the command of the senate, and who have often, when bringing home a victorious army, been given an audience outside the walls, you now, after slaughtering your countrymen, stained with the blood of your kindred, march into the city with standards erect. "Let liberty," say you, "be silent amidst the ensigns of war, and now that wars are driven far away and no ground for terror remains, let that people which conquered and civilized all nations be beleaguered within its own walls, and shudder at the sight of its own eagles."

XVI. Coriolanus was ungrateful, and became dutiful late, and after repenting of his crime; he did indeed lay down his arms, but only in the midst of his unnatural warfare. Catilina was ungrateful; he was not satisfied with taking his country captive without overturning it, without despatching the hosts of the Allobroges against it, without bringing an enemy from beyond the Alps to glut his old inborn hatred, and to offer Roman generals as sacrifices which had been long owing to the tombs of the Gaulish dead. Caius Marius was ungrateful, when, after being raised from the ranks to the consulship, he felt that he would not have wreaked his vengeance upon fortune, and would sink to his original obscurity, unless he slaughtered Romans as freely as he had slaughtered the Cimbri, and not merely gave the signal, but was himself the signal for civil disasters and butcheries. Lucius Sulla was ungrateful, for he saved his country by using remedies worse than the perils with which it was threatened, when he marched through human blood all the way from the citadel of Praeneste to the Colline Gate, fought more battles and caused more slaughter afterwards within the city, and most cruelly after the victory was won, most wickedly after quarter had been promised them, drove two legions into a corner and put them to the sword, and, great gods! invented a proscription by which he who slew a Roman citizen received indemnity, a sum of money, everything but a civic crown! Cnaeus Pompeius was ungrateful, for the return which he made to his country for three consulships, three triumphs, and the innumerable public offices into most of which he thrust himself when under age, was to lead others also to lay hands upon her under the pretext of thus rendering his own power less odious; as though what no one ought to do became right if more than one person did it. Whilst he was coveting extraordinary commands, arranging the provinces so as to have his own choice of them, and dividing the whole state with a third person, [Footnote: Crassus.] in such a manner as to leave two-thirds of it in the possession of his own family,

[Footnote: Pompey was married to Caesar's daughter. Cf. Virg., "Aen.," vi., 831, sq., and Lucan's beautiful verses, "Phars.," i., 114.] he reduced the Roman people to such a condition that they could only save themselves by submitting to slavery. The foe and conqueror [Footnote: Seneca is careful to avoid the mention of Caesar's name, which might have given offence to the emperors under whom he lived, who used the name as a title.] of Pompeius was himself ungrateful; he brought war from Gaul and Germany to Rome, and he, the friend of the populace, the champion of the commons, pitched his camp in the Circus Flaminus, nearer to the city than Porsena's camp had been. He did, indeed, use the cruel privileges of victory with moderation; as was said at the time, he protected his countrymen, and put to death no man who was not in arms. Yet what credit is there in this? Others used their arms more cruelly, but flung them away when glutted with blood, while he, though he soon sheathed the sword, never laid it aside. Antonius was ungrateful to his dictator, who he declared was rightly slain, and whose murderers he allowed to depart to their commands in the provinces; as for his country, after it had been torn to pieces by so many proscriptions, invasions, and civil wars, he intended to subject it to kings, not even of Roman birth, and to force that very state to pay tribute to eunuchs, [Footnote: The allusion is to Antonius's connection with Cleopatra. Cf. Virg. "Aen.," viii., 688.] which had itself restored sovereign rights, autonomy, and immunities, to the Achaeans, the Rhodians, and the people of many other famous cities.

XVII. The day would not be long enough for me to enumerate those who have pushed their ingratitude so far as to ruin their native land. It would be as vast a task to mention how often the state has been ungrateful to its best and most devoted lovers, although it has done no less wrong than it has suffered. It sent Camillus and Scipio into exile; even after the death of Catiline it exiled Cicero, destroyed his house, plundered his property, and did everything which Catiline would have done if victorious; Rutilius found his virtue rewarded with a hiding-place in Asia; to Cato the Roman people refused the praetorship, and persisted in refusing the consulship. We are ungrateful in public matters; and if every man asks himself, you will find that there is no one who has not some private ingratitude to complain of. Yet it is impossible that all men should complain, unless all were deserving of complaint, therefore all men are ungrateful. Are they ungrateful alone? nay, they are also all covetous, all spiteful, and all cowardly, especially those who appear daring; and, besides this, all men fawn upon the great, and all are impious. Yet you need not be angry with them; pardon them, for they are all mad. I do not wish to recall you to what is not proved, or to say, "See how ungrateful is youth! what young man, even if of innocent life, does not long for his father's death? even if moderate in his desires, does not look forward to it? even if dutiful, does not think about it? How few there are who fear the death even of the best of wives, who do not even calculate the probabilities of it. Pray, what litigant, after having been successfully defended, retains any remembrance of so great a benefit for more than a few days?" All agree that no one dies without complaining. Who on his last day dares to say,

"I've lived, I've done the task which Fortune set me."

Who does not leave the world with reluctance, and with lamentations? Yet it is the part of an ungrateful man not to be satisfied with the past. Your days will always be few if you count them. Reflect that length of time is not the greatest of blessings; make the best of your time, however short it may be; even if the day of your death be postponed, your happiness will not be increased, for life is merely made longer, not pleasanter, by delay. How much better is it to be thankful for the pleasures which one has received, not to reckon up the years of others, but to set a high value upon one's own, and score them to one's credit, saying, "God thought me worthy of this; I am satisfied with it; he might have given me more, but this, too, is a benefit." Let us be grateful towards both gods and men, grateful to those who have given us anything, and grateful even to those who have given anything to our relatives.

XVIII. "You render me liable to an infinite debt of gratitude," says our opponent, "when you say 'even to those who have given any thing to our relations,' so fix some limit. He who bestows a benefit upon the son, according to you, bestows it likewise upon the father: this is the first question I wish to raise. In the next place I should like to have a clear definition of whether a benefit, if it be bestowed upon your friend's father as well as upon himself, is bestowed also upon his brother? or upon his uncle? or his grandfather? or his wife and his father-in-law? tell me where I am to stop, how far I am to follow out the pedigree of the family?"

SENECA. If I cultivate your land, I bestow a benefit upon you; if I extinguish your house when burning, or prop it so as to save it from falling, I shall bestow a benefit upon you; if I heal your slave, I shall charge it to you; if I save your son's life, will you not thereby receive a benefit from me?

XIX. THE ADVERSARY. Your instances are not to the purpose, for he who cultivates my land, does not benefit the land, but me; he who props my house so that it does not fall, does this service to me, for the house itself is without feeling, and as it has none, it is I who am indebted to him; and he who cultivates my land does so because he wishes to oblige me, not to oblige the land. I should say the same of a slave; he is a chattel owned by me; he is saved for my advantage, therefore I am indebted for him. My son is himself capable of receiving a benefit; so it is he who receives it; I am gratified at a benefit which comes so near to myself, but am not laid under any obligation.

SE. Still I should like you, who say that you are under no obligation, to answer me this. The good health, the happiness, and the inheritance of a son are connected with his father; his father will be more happy if he keeps his son safe, and more unhappy if he loses him. What follows, then? when a man is made happier by me and is freed from the greatest danger of unhappiness, does he not receive a benefit?

AD. No, because there are some things which are bestowed upon others, and yet flow from them so as to reach ourselves; yet we must ask the person upon whom it was bestowed for repayment; as for example, money must be sought from the man to whom it was lent, although it may, by some means, have come into my hands. There is no benefit whose advantages do not extend to the receiver's nearest friends, and sometimes even to those less intimately connected with him; yet we do not enquire whither the benefit has proceeded from him to whom it was first given, but where it was first placed. You must demand repayment from the defendant himself personally.

SE. Well, but I pray you, do you not say, "you have preserved my son for me; had he perished, I could not have survived him?" Do you not owe a benefit for the life of one whose safety you value above your own? Moreover, should I save your son's life, you would fall down before my knees, and would pay vows to heaven as though you yourself had been saved; you would say, "It makes no difference whether you have saved mine or me; you have saved us both, yet me more than him." Why do you say this, if you do not receive a benefit?

A.D. Because, if my son were to contract a loan, I should pay his creditor, yet I should not, therefore, be indebted to him; or if my son were taken in adultery, I should blush, yet I should not, therefore, be an adulterer. I say that I am under an obligation to you for saving my son, not because I really am, but because I am willing to constitute myself your debtor of my own free will. On the other hand I have derived from his safety the greatest possible pleasure and advantage, and I have escaped that most dreadful blow, the loss of my child. True, but we are not now discussing whether you have done me any good or not, but whether you have bestowed a benefit upon me; for animals, stones, and herbs can do one good, but do not bestow benefits, which can only be given by one who wishes well to the receiver. Now you do not wish well to the father, but only to the son; and sometimes you do not even know the father. So when you have said, "Have I not bestowed a benefit upon the father by saving the son?" you ought to meet this with, "Have I, then, bestowed a benefit upon a father whom I do not know, whom I never thought of?" And what will you say when, as is sometimes the case, you hate the father, and yet save his son? Can you be thought to have bestowed a benefit upon one whom you hated most bitterly while you were bestowing it?

However, if I were to lay aside the bickering of dialogue, and answer you as a lawyer, I should say that you ought to consider the intention of the giver, you must regard his benefit as bestowed upon the person upon whom he meant to bestow it. If he did it in honour of the father, then the father received the benefit; if he thought only of the son, then the father is not laid under any obligation: by the benefit which was conferred upon the son, even though the father derives pleasure from it. Should he, however, have an opportunity, he will himself wish to give you something, yet not as though he were forced to repay a debt, but rather as if he had grounds for beginning an exchange of favours. No return for a benefit ought to be demanded from the father of the receiver; if he does you any kindness in return for it, he should be regarded as, a righteous man, but not as a grateful one. For there is no end to it; if I bestow a benefit on the receiver's father, do I likewise bestow it upon his mother, his grandfather, his maternal uncle, his children, relations, friends, slaves, and country? Where, then, does a benefit begin to stop? for there follows it this endless chain of people, to whom it is hard to assign bounds, because they join it by degrees, and are always creeping on towards it.

XX. A common question is, "Two brothers are at variance. If I save the life of one, do I confer a benefit upon the other, who will be sorry that his hated brother did not perish?" There can be no doubt that it is a benefit to do good to a man, even against that man's will, just as he, who against his own will does a man good, does not bestow a benefit upon him. "Do you," asks our adversary, "call that by which he is displeased and hurt a benefit?" Yes; many benefits have a harsh and forbidding appearance, such as cutting or burning to cure disease, or confining with chains. We must not consider whether a man is grieved at receiving a benefit, but whether he ought to rejoice: a coin is not bad because it is refused by a savage who is unacquainted with its proper stamp. A man receives a benefit even though he hates what is done, provided that it does him good, and that the giver bestowed it in order to do him good. It makes no difference if he receives a good thing in a bad spirit. Consider the converse of this. Suppose that a man hates his brother, though it is to his advantage to have a brother, and I kill this brother, this is not a benefit, though he may say that it is, and be glad of it. Our most artful enemies are those whom we thank for the wrongs which they do us.

"I understand; a thing which does good is a benefit, a thing which does harm is not a benefit. Now I will suggest to you an act which neither does good nor harm, and yet is a benefit. Suppose that I find the corpse of some one's father in a wilderness, and bury it, then I certainly have done him no good, for what difference could it make to him in what manner his body decayed? Nor have I done any good to his son, for what advantage does he gain by my act?" I will tell you what he gains. He has by my means performed a solemn and necessary rite; I have performed a service for his father which he would have wished, nay, which it would have been his duty to have performed himself. Yet this act is not a benefit, if I merely yielded to those feelings of pity and kindliness which would make me bury any corpse whatever, but only if I recognized this body, and buried it, with the thought in my mind that I was doing this service to the son; but, by merely throwing earth over a dead stranger, I lay no one under an obligation for an act performed on general principles of humanity.

It may be asked, "Why are you so careful in inquiring upon whom you bestow benefits, as though some day you meant to demand repayment of them? Some say that repayment should never be demanded; and they give the following reasons. An unworthy man will not repay the benefit which he has received, even if it be demanded of him, while a worthy man will do so of his own accord. Consequently, if you have bestowed it upon a good man, wait; do not outrage him by asking him for it, as though of his own accord he never would repay it. If you have bestowed it upon a bad man, suffer for it, but do not spoil your benefit by turning it into a loan. Moreover the law, by not authorizing you, forbids you, by implication, to demand the repayment of a benefit." All this is nonsense. As long as I am in no pressing need, as long as I am not forced by poverty, I will lose my benefits rather than ask for repayment; but if the lives of my children were at stake, if my wife were in danger, if my regard for the welfare of my country and for my own liberty were to force me to adopt a course which I disliked, I should overcome my delicacy, and openly declare that I had done all that I could to avoid the necessity of receiving help from an ungrateful man; the necessity of obtaining repayment of one's benefit will in the end overcome one's delicacy about asking for it. In the next place, when I bestow a benefit upon a good man, I do so with the intention of never demanding repayment, except in case of absolute necessity.

XXI. "But," argues he, "by not authorizing you, the law forbids you to exact repayment." There are many things which are not enforced by any law or process, but which the conventions of society, which are stronger than any law, compel us to observe. There is no law forbidding us to divulge our friend's secrets; there is no law which bids us keep faith even with an enemy; pray what law is there which binds us to stand by what we have promised? There is none. Nevertheless I should remonstrate with one who did not keep a secret, and I should be indignant with one who pledged his word and broke it. "But," he argues, "you are turning a benefit into a loan." By no means, for I do not insist upon repayment, but only demand it; nay, I do not even demand it, but remind my friend of it. Even the direst need will not bring me to apply for help to one with whom I should have to undergo a long struggle.

If there be any one so ungrateful that it is not sufficient to remind him of his debt, I should pass him over, and think that he did not deserve to be made grateful by force. A money-lender does not demand repayment from his debtors if he knows they have become bankrupt, and, to their shame, have nothing but shame left to lose; and I, like him, should pass over those who are openly and obstinately ungrateful, and would demand repayment only from those who were likely to give it me, not from those from whom I should have to extort it by force.

XXII. There are many who cannot deny that they have received a benefit, yet cannot return it—men who are not good enough to be termed grateful, nor yet bad enough to be termed ungrateful; but who are dull and sluggish, backward debtors, though not defaulters. Such men as these I should not ask for repayment, but forcibly remind them of it, and, from a state of indifference, bring them back to their duty. They would at once reply, "Forgive me; I did not know, by Hercules, that you missed this, or I would have offered it of my own accord, I beg that you will not think me ungrateful; I remember your goodness to me." Why need I hesitate to make such men as these better to themselves and to me? I would prevent any one from doing wrong, if I were able; much more would I prevent a friend, both lest he should do wrong, and lest he should do wrong to me in particular. I bestow a second benefit upon him by not permitting him to be ungrateful; and I should not reproach him harshly with what I had done for him, but should speak as gently as I could. In order to afford him an opportunity of returning my kindness, I should refresh his remembrance of it, and ask for a benefit; he would understand that I was asking for repayment. Sometimes I would make use of somewhat severe language, if I had any hope that by it he might be amended; though I would not irritate a hopelessly ungrateful man, for fear that I might turn him into an enemy. If we spare the ungrateful even the affront of reminding them of their conduct, we shall render them' more backward in returning benefits; and although some might be cured of their evil ways, and be made into good men, if their consciences were stung by remorse, yet we shall allow them to perish for want of a word of warning, with which a father sometimes corrects his son, a wife brings back to herself an erring husband, or a man stimulates the wavering fidelity of his friend.

XXIII. To awaken some men, it is only necessary to stir them, not to strike them; in like manner, with some men, the feeling of honour about returning a benefit is not extinct, but slumbering. Let us rouse it. "Do not," they will say, "make the kindness you have done me into a wrong: for it is a wrong, if you do not demand some return from me, and so make me ungrateful. What if I do not know what sort of repayment you wish for? if I am so occupied by business, and my attention is so much diverted to other subjects that I have not been able to watch for an opportunity of serving you? Point out to me what I can do for you, what you wish me to do. Why do you despair, before making a trial of me? Why are you in such haste to lose both your benefit and your friend? How can you tell whether I do not wish, or whether I do not know how to repay you: whether it be in intention or in opportunity that I am wanting? Make a trial of me." I would therefore remind him of what I had done, without bitterness, not in public, or in a reproachful manner, but so that he may think that he himself has remembered it rather than that it has been recalled to him.

XXIV. One of Julius Caesar's veterans was once pleading before him against his neighbours, and the cause was going against him. "Do you remember, general," said he, "that in Spain you dislocated your ankle near the river Sucro [Footnote: Xucar]?" When Caesar said that he remembered it, he continued, "Do you remember that when, during the excessive heat, you wished to rest under a tree which afforded very little shade, as the ground in which that solitary tree grew was rough and rocky, one of your comrades spread his cloak under you?" Caesar answered, "Of course, I remember; indeed, I was perishing with thirst; and since was unable to walk to the nearest spring, I would have crawled thither on my hands and knees, had not my comrade, a brave and active man, brought me water in his helmet." "Could you, then, my general, recognize that man or that helmet?" Caesar replied that he could not remember the helmet, but that he could remember the man well; and he added, I fancy in anger at being led away to this old story in the midst of a judicial enquiry, "At any rate, you are not he." "I do not blame you, Caesar," answered the man, "for not recognizing me; for when this took place, I was unwounded; but afterwards, at the battle of Munda, my eye was struck out, and the bones of my skull crushed. Nor would you recognize that helmet if you saw it, for it was split by a Spanish sword." Caesar would not permit this man to be troubled with lawsuits, and presented his old soldier with the fields through which a village right of way had given rise to the dispute.

XXV. In this case, what ought he to have done? Because his commander's memory was confused by a multitude of incidents, and because his position as the leader of vast armies did not permit him to notice individual soldiers, ought the man not to have asked for a return for the benefit which he had conferred? To act as he did is not so much to ask for a return as to take it when it lies in a convenient position ready for us, although we have to stretch out our hands in order to receive it. I shall therefore ask for the return of a benefit, whenever I am either reduced to great straits, or where by doing so I shall act to the advantage of him from whom I ask it. Tiberius Caesar, when some one addressed him with the words, "Do you remember....?" answered, before the man could mention any further proofs of former acquaintance, "I do not remember what I was." Why should it not be forbidden to demand of this man repayment of former favours? He had a motive for forgetting them: he denied all knowledge of his friends and comrades, and wished men only to see, to think, and to speak of him as emperor. He regarded his old friend as an impertinent meddler.

We ought to be even more careful to choose a favorable opportunity when we ask for a benefit to be repaid to us than when we ask for one to be bestowed upon us. We must be temperate in our language, so that the grateful may not take offence, or the ungrateful pretend to do so. If we lived among wise men, it would be our duty to wait in silence until our benefits were returned. Yet even to wise men it would be better to give some hint of what our position required. We ask for help even from the gods themselves, from whose knowledge nothing is hid, although our prayers cannot alter their intentions towards us, but can only recall them to their minds. Homer's priest, [Il. i. 39

sqq.] I say, recounts even to the gods his duteous conduct and his pious care of their altars. The second best form of virtue is to be willing and able to take advice.[Hes. Op. 291.] A horse who is docile and prompt to obey can be guided hither and thither by the slightest movement of the reins. Very few men are led by their own reason: those who come next to the best are those who return to the right path in consequence of advice; and these we must not deprive of their guide. When our eyes are covered they still possess sight; but it is the light of day which, when admitted to them, summons them to perform their duty: tools lie idle, unless the workman uses them to take part in his work. Similarly men's minds contain a good feeling, which, however, lies torpid, either through luxury and disuse, or through ignorance of its duties. This we ought to render useful, and not to get into a passion with it, and leave it in its wrong doing, but bear with it patiently, just as schoolmasters bear patiently with the blunders of forgetful scholars; for as by the prompting of a word or two their memory is often recalled to the text of the speech which they have to repeat, so men's goodwill can be brought to return kindness by reminding them of it.

BOOK VI.

I.

There are some things, my most excellent Liberalis, which lie completely outside of our actual life, and which we only inquire into in order to exercise our intellects, while others both give us pleasure while we are discovering them, and are of use when discovered. I will place all these in your hands; you, at your own discretion, may order them either to be investigated thoroughly, or to be reserved, and be used as agreeable interludes. Something will be gained even by those which you dismiss at once, for it is advantageous even to know what subjects are not worth learning. I shall be guided, therefore, by your face: according to its expression, I shall deal with some questions at greater length, and drive others out of court, and put an end to them at once.

II. It is a question whether a benefit can be taken away from one by force. Some say that it cannot, because it is not a thing, but an act. A gift is not the same as the act of giving, any more than a sailor is the same as the act of sailing. A sick man and a disease are not the same thing, although no one can be ill without disease; and, similarly, a benefit itself is one thing, and what any of us receive through a benefit is another. The benefit itself is incorporeal, and never becomes invalid; but its subject-matter changes owners, and passes from hand to hand. So, when you take away from anyone what you have given him, you take away the subject-matter only of the benefit, not the benefit itself. Nature herself cannot recall what she has given. She may cease to bestow benefits, but cannot take them away: a man who dies, yet has lived; a man who becomes blind, nevertheless has seen. She can cut off her blessings from us in the future, but she cannot prevent our having enjoyed them in the past. We are frequently not able to enjoy a benefit for long, but the benefit is not thereby destroyed. Let Nature struggle as hard as she please, she cannot give herself retrospective action. A man may lose his house, his money, his property—everything to which the name of benefit can be given—yet the benefit itself will remain firm and unmoved; no power can prevent his benefactor's having bestowed them, or his having received them.

III. I think that a fine passage in Rabirius's poem, where M. Antonius, seeing his fortune deserting him, nothing left him except the privilege of dying, and even that only on condition that he used it promptly, exclaims,

"What I have given, that I now possess!"

How much he might have possessed, had he chosen! These are riches to be depended upon, which through all the turmoil of human life will remain steadfast; and the greater they are, the less envy they will attract. Why are you sparing of your property, as though it were your own? You are but the manager of it. All those treasures, which make you swell with pride, and soar above mere mortals, till you forget the weakness of your nature; all that which you lock up in iron-grated treasuries, and guard in arms, which you win from other men with their lives, and defend at the risk of your own; for which you launch fleets to dye the sea with blood, and shake the walls of cities, not knowing what arrows fortune may be preparing for you behind your back; to gain which you have so often violated all the ties of relationship, of friendship, and of colleagueship, till the whole world lies crushed between the two combatants: all these are not yours; they are a kind of deposit, which is on the point of passing into other hands: your enemies, or your heirs, who are little better, will seize upon them. "How," do you ask, "can you make them your own?" "By giving them away." Do, then, what is best for your own interests, and gain a sure enjoyment of them, which cannot be taken from you, making them at once more certainly yours, and more honorable to you. That which you esteem so highly, that by which you think that you are made rich and powerful, owns but the shabby title of "house," "slave," or "money;" but when you have given it away, it becomes a benefit.

IV. "You admit," says our adversary, "that we sometimes are under no obligation to him from whom we have received a benefit. In that case it has been taken by force." Nay, there are many things which would cause us to cease to feel gratitude for a benefit, not because the benefit has been taken from me, but because it has been spoiled. Suppose that a man has defended me in a lawsuit, but has forcibly outraged my wife; he has not taken away the benefit which he conferred upon me, but by balancing it with an equivalent wrong, he has set me free from my debt; indeed, if he has injured me more than he had previously benefited me, he not only puts an end to my gratitude, but makes me free to revenge myself upon him, and to complain of him, when the wrong outweighs the benefit; in such a case the benefit is not taken away, but is overcome. Why, are not some fathers so cruel and so wicked that it is right and proper for their sons to turn away from them, and disown them? Yet, pray, have they taken away the life which they gave? No, but their unnatural conduct in later years has destroyed all the gratitude which was due to them for their original benefit. In these cases it is not a benefit itself, but the gratitude owing for a benefit which is taken away, and the result is, not that one does not possess the benefit, but that one is not laid under any obligation by it. It is as though a man were to lend me money, and then burn my house down; the advantage of the loan is balanced by the damage which he has caused: I do not repay him, and yet I am not in his debt. In like manner any one who may have acted kindly and generously to me, and who afterwards has shown himself haughty, insulting, and cruel, places me in just the same position as though I never had received anything from him: he has murdered his own benefits. Though the lease may remain in force, still a man does not continue to be a tenant if his landlord tramples down his crops, or cuts down his orchard; their contract is at an end, not because the landlord has received the rent which was agreed upon, but because he has made it impossible that he should receive it. So, too, a creditor often has to pay money to his debtor, should he have taken more property from him in other transactions than he claims as having lent him. The judge does not sit merely to decide between debtor and creditor, when he says, "You did lend the man money; but then, what followed? You have driven away his cattle, you have murdered his slave, you have in your possession plate which you have not paid for. After valuing what each has received, I order you, who came to this court as a creditor, to leave it as a debtor." In like manner a balance is struck between benefits and injuries. In many cases, I repeat, a benefit is not taken away from him who receives it, and yet it lays him under no obligation, if the giver has repented of giving it, called himself unhappy because he gave it, sighed or made a wry face while he gave it; if he thought that he was throwing it away rather than giving it, if he gave it to please himself, or to please any one except me, the receiver; if he persistently makes himself offensive by boasting of what he has done, if he brags of his gift everywhere, and makes it a misery to me, then indeed the benefit remains in my hands, but I owe him nothing for it, just as sums of money to which a creditor has no legal right are owed to him, but cannot be claimed by him.

V. Though you have bestowed a benefit upon me, yet you have since done me a wrong; the benefit demanded gratitude, the wrong required vengeance: the result is that I do not owe you gratitude, nor do you owe me compensation—each is cancelled by the other. When we say, "I returned him his benefit," we do not mean that we restored to him the very thing which we had received, but something else in its place. To return is to give back one thing instead of another, because, of course, in all repayment it is not the thing itself, but its equivalent which is returned. We are said to have returned money even though we count out gold pieces instead of silver ones, or even if no money passes between us, but the transaction be effected verbally by the assignment of a debt.

I think I see you say, "You are wasting your time; of what use is it to me to know whether what I do not owe to another still remains in my hands or not? These are like the ingenious subtleties of the lawyers, who declare that one cannot acquire an inheritance by prescription, but can only acquire those things of which the inheritance consists, as though there were any difference between the heritage and the things of which it consists. Rather decide this point for me, which may be of use. If the same man confers a benefit upon me, and afterwards does me a wrong, is it my duty to return the benefit to him, and nevertheless to avenge myself upon him, having, as it were, two distinct accounts open with him, or to mix them both together, and do nothing, leaving the benefit to be wiped out by the injury, the injury by the benefit? I see that the former course is adopted by the law of the land; you know best what the law may be among you Stoic philosophers in such a case. I suppose that you keep the action which I bring against another distinct from that which he Strings against me, and the two processes are not merged into one? For instance, if a man entrusts me with money, and afterwards robs me, I shall bring an action against him for theft, and he will bring one against me for unlawfully detaining his property?"

VI. The cases which you have mentioned, my Liberalis, come under well-established laws, which it is necessary for us to follow. One law cannot be merged in another: each one proceeds its own way. There is a particular action which deals with deposits just as there is one which deals with theft. A benefit is subject to no law; it depends upon my own arbitration. I am at liberty to contrast the amount of good or harm which any one may have done me, and then to decide which of us is indebted to the other. In legal processes we ourselves have no power, we must go whither they lead us; in the case of a benefit the supreme power is mine, I pronounce sentence. Consequently I do not separate or distinguish between benefits and wrongs, but send them before the same judge. Unless I did so, you would bid me love and hate, give thanks and make complaints at the same time, which human nature does not admit of. I would rather compare the benefit and the injury with one another, and see whether there were any balance in my favour. If anybody puts lines of other writing upon my manuscript he conceals, though he does not take away, the letters which were there before, and in like manner a wrong coming after a benefit does not allow it to be seen.

VII. Your face, by which I have agreed to be guided, now becomes wrinkled with frowns, as though I were straying too widely from the subject. You seem to say to me:

"Why steer to seaward?
Hither bend thy course,
Hug close the shore..."

I do hug it as close as possible. So now, if you think that we have dwelt sufficiently upon this point, let us proceed to the consideration of the next—that is, whether we are at all indebted to any one who does us good without wishing to do so. I might have expressed this more clearly, if it were not right that the question should be somewhat obscurely stated, in order that by the distinction immediately following it may be shown that we mean to investigate the case both of him who does us good against his will, and that of him who does us good without knowing it. That a man who does us good by acting under compulsion does not thereby lay us under any obligation, is so clear, that no words are needed to prove it. Both this question, and any other of the like character which may be raised, can easily be settled if in each case we bear in mind that, for anything to be a benefit, it must reach us in the first place through some thought, and secondly through the thought of a friend and well-wisher. Therefore we do not feel any gratitude towards rivers, albeit they may bear large ships, afford an ample and unvarying stream for the conveyance of merchandise, or flow beauteously and full of fish through fertile fields. No one conceives himself to be indebted for a benefit to the Nile, any more than he would owe it a grudge if its waters flooded his fields to excess, and retired more slowly than usual; the wind does not bestow benefits, gentle and favorable though it may be, nor does wholesome and useful food; for he who would bestow a benefit upon me, must not only do me good, but must wish to do so. No obligation can therefore be incurred towards dumb animals; yet how many men have been saved from peril by the swiftness of a horse!—nor yet towards trees—yet how many sufferers from summer heat have been sheltered by the thick foliage of a tree! What difference can it make, whether I have profited by the act of one who did not know that he was doing me good, or one who could not know it, when in each case the will to do me good was wanting? You might as well bid me be grateful to a ship, a carriage, or a lance for saving me from danger, as bid me be grateful to a man who may have done me good by chance, but with no more intention of doing me good than those things could have.

VIII. Some men may receive benefits without knowing it, but no man can bestow them without knowing it. Many sick persons have been cured by chance circumstances, which do not therefore become specific remedies; as, for instance, one man was restored to health by falling into a river during very cold weather, as another was set free from a quartan fever by means of a flogging, because the sudden terror turned his attention into a new channel, so that the dangerous hours passed unnoticed. Yet none of these are remedies, even though they may have been successful; and in like manner some men do us good, though they are unwilling—indeed, because they are unwilling to do so—yet we need not feel grateful to them as though we had received a benefit from them, because fortune has changed the evil which they intended into good. Do you suppose that I am indebted to a man who strikes my enemy with a blow which he aimed at me, who would have injured me had he not missed his mark? It often happens that by openly perjuring himself a man makes even trustworthy witnesses disbelieved, and renders his intended victim an object of compassion, as though he were being ruined by a conspiracy. Some have been saved by the very power which was exerted to crush them, and judges who would have condemned a man by law, have refused to condemn him by favour. Yet they did not confer a benefit upon the accused, although they rendered him a service, because we must consider at what the dart was aimed, not what it hits, and a benefit is distinguished from an injury not by its result, but by the spirit in which it was meant. By contradicting himself, by irritating the judge by his arrogance, or by rashly allowing his whole case to depend upon the testimony of one witness, my opponent may have saved my cause. I do not consider whether his mistakes benefited me or not, for he wished me ill.

IX. In order that I may be grateful, I must wish to do what my benefactor must have wished in order that he might bestow a benefit. Can anything be more unjust than to bear a grudge against a person who may have trodden upon one's foot in a crowd, or splashed one, or pushed one the way which one did not wish to go? Yet it was by his act that we were injured, and we only refrain from complaining of him, because he did not know what he was doing. The same reason makes it possible for men to do us good without conferring benefits upon us, or to harm us without doing us wrong, because it is intention which distinguishes our friends from our enemies. How many have been saved from service in the army by sickness! Some men have been saved from sharing the fall of their house, by being brought up upon their recognizances to a court of law by their enemies; some have been saved by ship-wreck from falling into the hands of pirates; yet we do not feel grateful to such things, because chance has no feeling of the service it renders, nor are we grateful to our enemy, though his lawsuit, while it harassed and detained us, still saved our lives. Nothing can be a benefit which does not proceed from good will, and which is not meant as such by the giver. If any one does me a service, without knowing it, I am under no obligation to him; should he do so, meaning to injure me, I shall imitate his conduct.

X. Let us turn our attention to the first of these. Can you desire me to do anything to express my gratitude to a man who did nothing in order to confer a benefit upon me? Passing on to the next, do you wish me to show my gratitude to such a man, and of my own will to return to him what I received from him against his will? What am I to say of the third, he who, meaning to do an injury, blunders into bestowing a benefit? That you should have wished to confer a benefit upon me is not sufficient to render me grateful; but that you should have wished not to do so is enough to set me free from any obligation to you. A mere wish does not constitute a benefit; and just as the best and heartiest wish is not a benefit when fortune prevents its being carried into effect, neither is what fortune bestows upon us a benefit, unless good wishes preceded it. In order to lay me under an obligation, you must not merely do me a service, but you must do so intentionally.

XI. Cleanthes makes use of the following example:—"I sent," says he, "two slaves to look for Plato and bring him to me from the Academy. One of them searched through the whole of the colonnade, and every other place in which he thought that he was likely to be found, and returned home alike weary and unsuccessful; the other sat down among the audience of a mountebank close by, and, while amusing himself in the society of other slaves like a careless vagabond as he was, found Plato, without seeking for him, as he happened to pass that way. We ought," says he, "to praise that slave who, as far as lay in his power, did what he was ordered, and we ought to punish the other whose laziness turned out so fortunate." It is goodwill alone which does one real service; let us then consider under what conditions it lays us under obligations. It is not enough to wish a man well, without doing him good; nor is it enough to do him good without wishing him well. Suppose that some one wished to give me a present, but did not give it; I have his good will, but I do not have his benefit, which consists of subject matter and goodwill together. I owe nothing to one who wished to lend me money but did not do so, and in like manner I shall be the friend of one who wished but was not able to bestow a benefit upon me, but I shall not be under any obligation to him. I also shall wish to bestow something upon him, even as he did upon me; but if fortune be more favorable to me than to him, and I succeed in bestowing something upon him, my doing so will be a benefit bestowed upon him, not a repayment out of gratitude for what he did for me. It will become his duty to be grateful to me; I shall have begun the interchange of benefits; the series must be counted from my act.

XII. I already understand what you wish to ask; there is no need for you to say anything, your countenance speaks for you. "If any one does us good for his own sake, are we," you ask, "under an obligation to him? I often hear you complain that there are some things which men make use of themselves, but which they put down to the account of others." I will tell you, my Liberalis; but first let me distinguish between the two parts of your question, and separate what is fair from what is unfair. It makes a great difference whether any one bestows a benefit upon us for his own sake, or whether he does so partly for his own sake and partly for ours. He who looks only to his own interests, and who does us good because he cannot otherwise make a profit for himself, seems to me to be like the farmer who provides winter and summer fodder for his flocks, or like the man who feeds up the captives whom he has bought in order that they may fetch a better price in the slave market, or who crams and curry-combs fat oxen for sale; or like the keeper of a school of arms, who takes great pains in exercising and equipping his gladiators. As Cleanthes says, there is a great difference between benefits and trade.

XIII. On the other hand, I am not so unjust as to feel no gratitude to a man, because, while helping me, he helped himself also; for I do not insist upon his consulting my interests to the exclusion of his own—nay, I should prefer that the benefit which I receive may be of even greater advantage to the giver, provided that he thought of us both when giving it, and meant to divide it between me and himself. Even should he possess the larger portion of it, still, if he admits me to a share, if he meant it for both of us, I am not only unjust but ungrateful, if I do not rejoice in what has benefited me benefiting him also. It is the essence of spitefulness to say that nothing can be a benefit which does not cause some inconvenience to the giver.

As for him who bestows a benefit for his own sake, I should say to him, "You have made use of me, and how can you say that you have bestowed a benefit upon me, rather than I upon you?" "Suppose," answers he, "that I cannot obtain a public office except by ransoming ten citizens out of a great number of captives, will you owe me nothing for setting you free from slavery and bondage? Yet I shall do so for my own sake." To this I should answer, "You do this partly for my sake, partly for your own. It is for your own sake that you ransom captives, but it is for my sake that you ransom me; for to serve your purpose it would be enough for you to ransom any one. I am therefore your debtor, not for ransoming me but for choosing me, since you might have attained the same result by ransoming some one else instead of me. You divide the advantages of the act between yourself and me, and you confer upon me a benefit by which both of us profit. What you do entirely for my sake is, that you choose me in preference to others. If therefore you were to be made·praetor for ransoming ten captives, and there were only ten of us captives, none of us would be under any obligation to you, because there is nothing for which you can ask any one of us to give you credit apart from your own advantage. I do not regard a benefit jealously and wish it to be given to myself alone, but I wish to have a share in it."

XIV. "Well, then," says he, "suppose that I were to order all your names to be put into a ballot-box, and that your name was drawn among those who were to be ransomed, would you owe me nothing?" Yes, I should owe you something, but very little: how little, I will explain to you. By so doing you do something for my sake, in that you grant me the chance of being ransomed; I owe to fortune that my name was drawn, all I owe to you is that my name could be drawn. You have given me the means of obtaining your benefit. For the greater part of that benefit I am indebted to fortune; that I could be so indebted, I owe to you.

I shall take no notice whatever of those whose benefits are bestowed in a mercenary spirit, who do not consider to whom, but upon what terms they give, whose benefits are entirely selfish. Suppose that some one sells me corn; I cannot live unless I buy it; yet I do not owe my life to him because I have bought it. I do not consider how essential it was to me, and that I could not live without it; but how little thanks are due for it, since I could not have had it without paying for it, and since the merchant who imported it did not consider how much good he would do me, but how much he would gain for himself, I owe nothing for what I have bought and paid for.

XV. "According to this reasoning," says my opponent, "you would say that you owe nothing to a physician beyond his paltry fee, nor to your teacher, because you have paid him some money; yet these persons are all held very dear, and are very much respected." In answer to this I should urge that some things are of greater value than the price which we pay for them. You buy of a physician life and good health, the value of which cannot be estimated in money; from a teacher of the liberal sciences you buy the education of a gentleman and mental culture; therefore you pay these persons the price, not of what they give us, but of their trouble in giving it; you pay them for devoting their attention to us, for disregarding their own affairs to attend to us: they receive the price, not of their services, but of the expenditure of their time. Yet this may be more truly stated in another way, which I will at once lay before you, having first pointed out how the above may be confuted. Our adversary would say, "If some things are of greater value than the price which we pay for them, then, though you may have bought them, you still owe me something more for them." I answer, in the first place, what does their real value matter, since the buyer and seller have settled the price between them? Next, I did not buy it at it's own price, but at yours. "It is," you say, "worth more than its sale price." True, but it cannot be sold for more. The price of everything varies according to circumstances; after you have well praised your wares, they are worth only the highest price at which you can sell them; a man who buys things cheap is not on that account under any obligation to the seller. In the next place, even if they are worth more, there is no generosity in your letting them go for less, since the price is settled by custom and the rate of the market, not by the uses and powers of the merchandise. What would you state to be the proper payment of a man who crosses the seas, holding a true course through the midst of the waves after the land has sunk out of sight, who foresees coming storms, and suddenly, when no one expects danger, orders sails to be furled, yards to be lowered, and the crew to stand at their posts ready to meet the fury of the unexpected gale? and yet the price of such great skill is fully paid for by the passage money. At what sum can you estimate the value of a lodging in a wilderness, of a shelter in the rain, of a bath or fire in cold weather? Yet I know on what terms I shall be supplied with these when I enter an inn. How much the man does for us who props our house when it is about to fall, and who, with a skill beyond belief, suspends in the air a block of building which has begun to crack at the foundation; yet we can contract for underpinning at a fixed and cheap rate. The city wall keeps us safe from our enemies, and from sudden inroads of brigands; yet it is, well known how much a day a smith would earn for erecting towers and scaffoldings [Footnote: See Viollet-le-Duc's "Dictionnaire d'Architecture," articles "Architecture Militaire" and "Hourds," for the probable meaning of "Propugnacula."]to provide for the public safety.

XVI. I might go on for ever collecting instances to prove that valuable things are sold at a low price. What then? why is it that I owe something extra both to my physician and to my teacher, and that I do not acquit myself of all obligation to them by paying them their fee? It is because they pass from physicians and teachers into friends, and lay us under obligations, not by the skill which they sell to us, but by kindly and familiar good will. If my physician does no more than feel my pulse and class me among those whom he sees in his daily rounds, pointing out what I ought to do or to avoid without any personal interest, then I owe him no more than his fee, because he views me with the eye not of a friend, but of a commander. [Footnote: I read "Nbn tamquam amicus videt sed tamquam imperator."] Neither have I any reason for loving my teacher, if he has regarded me merely as one of the mass of his scholars, and has not thought me worthy of taking especial pains with by myself, if he has never fixed his attention upon me, and if when he discharged his knowledge on the public, I might be said rather to have picked it up than to have learnt it from him. What then is our reason for owing them much? It is, not that what they have sold us is worth more than we paid for it, but that they have given something to us personally. Suppose that my physician has spent more consideration upon my case than was professionally necessary; that it was for me, not for his own credit, that he feared: that he was not satisfied with pointing out remedies, but himself applied them, that he sat by my bedside among my anxious friends, and came to see me at the crises of my disorder; that no service was too troublesome or too disgusting for him to perform; that he did not hear my groans unmoved; that among the numbers who called for him I was his favourite case; and that he gave the others only so much time as his care of my health permitted him: I should feel obliged to such a man not as to a physician, but as to a friend. Suppose again that my teacher endured labour and weariness in instructing me; that he taught me something more than is taught by all masters alike; that he roused my better feelings by his encouragement, and that at one time he would raise my spirits by praise, and at another warn me to shake off slothfulness: that he laid his hand, as it were, upon my latent and torpid powers of intellect and drew them out into the light of day; that he did not stingily dole out to me what he knew, in order that he might be wanted for a longer time, but was eager, if possible, to pour all his learning into me; then I am ungrateful, if I do not love him as much as I love my nearest relatives and my dearest friends.

XVII. We give something additional even to those who teach the meanest trades, if their efforts appear to be extraordinary; we bestow a gratuity upon pilots, upon workmen who deal with the commonest materials and hire themselves out by the day. In the noblest arts, however, those which either preserve or beautify our lives, a man would be ungrateful who thinks he owes the artist no more than he bargained for. Besides this, the teaching of such learning as we have spoken of blends mind with mind; now when this takes place, both in the case of the physician and of the teacher the price of his work is paid, but that of his mind remains owing.

XVIII. Plato once crossed a river, and as the ferryman did not ask him for anything, he supposed that he had let him pass free out of respect, and said that the ferryman had laid Plato under an obligation. Shortly afterwards, seeing the ferryman take one person after another across the river with the same pains, and without charging anything, Plato declared that the ferryman had not laid him under an obligation. If you wish me to be grateful for what you give, you must not merely give it to me, but show that you mean it specially for me; you cannot make any claim upon one for having given him what you fling away broadcast among the crowd. What then? shall I owe you nothing for it? Nothing, as an individual; I will pay, when the rest of mankind do, what I owe no more than they.

XIX. "Do you say," inquires my opponent, "that he who carries me gratis in a boat across the river Po, does not bestow any benefit upon me?" I do. He does me some good, but he does not bestow a benefit upon me; for he does it for his own sake, or at any rate not for mine; in short, he himself does not imagine that he is bestowing a benefit upon me, but does it for the credit of the State, or of the neighbourhood, or of himself, and expects some return for doing so, different from what he would receive from individual passengers. "Well," asks my opponent, "if the emperor were to grant the franchise to all the Gauls, or exemption, from taxes to all the Spaniards, would each individual of them owe him nothing on that account?" Of course he would: but he would be indebted to him, not as having personally received a benefit intended for himself alone, but as a partaker in one conferred upon his nation. He would argue, "The emperor had no thought of me at the time when he benefited us all; he did not care to give me the franchise separately, he did not fix his attention upon me; why then should I be grateful to one who did not have me in his mind when he was thinking of doing what he did? In answer to this, I say that when he thought of doing good to all the Gauls, he thought of doing good to me also, for I was a Gaul, and he included me under my national, if not under my personal appellation. In like manner, I should feel grateful to him, not as for a personal, but for a general benefit; being only one of the people, I should regard the debt of gratitude as incurred, not by myself, but by my country, and should not pay it myself, but only contribute my share towards doing so. I do not call a man my creditor because he has lent money to my country, nor should I include that money in a schedule of my debts were I either a candidate for a public office, or a defendant in the courts; yet I would pay my share towards extinguishing such a debt. Similarly, I deny that I am laid under an obligation by a gift bestowed upon my entire nation, because although the giver gave it to me, yet he did not do so for my sake, but gave it without knowing whether he was giving it to me or not: nevertheless I should feel that I owed something for the gift, because it did reach me, though not directly. To lay me under an obligation, a thing must be done for my sake alone."

XX. "According to this," argues our opponent, "you are under no obligation to the sun or the moon; for they do not move for your sake alone." No, but since they move with the object of preserving the balance of the universe, they move for my sake also, seeing that I am a fraction of the universe. Besides, our position and theirs is not the same, for he who does me good in order that he may by my means do good to himself, does not bestow a benefit upon me, because he merely makes use of me as an instrument for his own advantage; whereas the sun and the moon, even if they do us good for their own sakes, still cannot do good to us in order that by our means they may do good to themselves, for what is there which we can bestow upon them?

XXI. "I should be sure," replies he, "that the sun and the moon wished to do us good, if they were able to refuse to do so; but they cannot help moving as they do. In short, let them stop and discontinue their work."

See now, in how many ways this argument may be refuted. One who cannot refuse to do a thing may nevertheless wish to do it; indeed there is no greater proof of a fixed desire to do anything, than not to be able to alter one's determination. A good man cannot leave undone what he does: for unless he does it he will not be a good man. Is a good man, then, not able to bestow a benefit, because he does what he ought to do, and is not able not to do what he ought to do? Besides this, it makes a great difference whether you say, "He is not able not to do this, because he is forced to do it," or "He is not able to wish not to do it;" for, if he could not help doing it, then I am not indebted for it to him, but to the person who forced him to do it; if he could not help wishing for it because he had nothing better to wish for, then it is he who forces himself to do it, and in this case the debt which as acting under compulsion he could not claim, is due to him as compelling himself.

"Let the sun and moon cease to wish to benefit us," says our adversary. I answer, "Remember what has been said. Who can be so crazy as to refuse the name of free-will to that which has no danger of ceasing to act, and of adopting the opposite course, since, on the contrary, he whose will is fixed for ever, must be thought to wish more earnestly than any one else. Surely if he, who may at any moment change his mind, can be said to wish, we must not deny the existence of will in a being whose nature does not admit of change of mind."

XXII. "Well," says he "let them stop, if it be possible." What you say is this:—"Let all those heavenly bodies, placed as they are at vast distances from each other, and arranged to preserve the balance of the universe, leave their appointed posts: let sudden confusion arise, so that constellations may collide with constellations, that the established harmony of all things may be destroyed and the works of God be shaken into ruin; let the whole frame of the rapidly moving heavenly bodies abandon in mid career those movements which we were assured would endure for ages, and let those which now by their regular advance and retreat keep the world at a moderate temperature, be instantly consumed by fire, so that instead of the infinite variety of the seasons all may be reduced to one uniform condition; let fire rage everywhere, followed by dull night, and let the bottomless abyss swallow up all the gods." Is it worth while to destroy all this merely in order to refute you? Even though you do not wish it, they do you good, and they wheel in their courses for your sake, though their motion may be due to some earlier and more important cause.

XXIII. Besides this, the gods act under no external constraint, but their own will is a law to them for all time. They have established an order which is not to be changed, and consequently it is impossible that they should appear to be likely to do anything against their will, since they wish to continue doing whatever they cannot cease from doing, and they never regret their original decision, No doubt it is impossible for them to stop short, or to desert to the other side, but it is so for no other reason than that their own force holds them to their purpose. It is from no weakness that they persevere; no, they have no mind to leave the best course, and by this it is fated that they should proceed. When, at the time of the original creation, they arranged the entire universe, they paid attention to us as well as to the rest, and took thought about the human race; and for this reason we cannot suppose that it is merely for their own pleasure that they move in their orbits and display their work since we also are a part of that work. We are, therefore; under an obligation to the sun and moon and the rest of the heavenly host, because, although they may rise in order to bestow more important benefits than those which we receive from them, yet they do bestow these upon us as they pass on their way to greater things. Besides this, they assist us of set purpose, and, therefore, lay us under an obligation, because we do not in their case stumble by chance upon a benefit bestowed by one who knew not what he was doing, but they knew that we should receive from them the advantages which we do; so that, though they may have some higher aim, though the result of their movements may be something of greater importance than the preservation of the human race, yet from the beginning thought has been directed to our comforts, and the scheme of the world has been arranged in a fashion which proves that our interests were neither their least nor last concern. It is our duty to show filial love for our parents, although many of them had no thought of children when they married. Not so with the gods: they cannot but have known what they were doing when they furnished mankind with food and comforts. Those for whose advantage so much was created, could not have been created without design. Nature conceived the idea of us before she formed us, and, indeed, we are no such trifling piece of work as could have fallen from her hands unheeded. See how great privileges she has bestowed upon us, how far beyond the human race the empire of mankind extends; consider how widely she allows us to roam, not having restricted us to the land alone, but permitted us to traverse every part of herself; consider, too, the audacity of our intellect, the only one which knows of the gods or seeks for them, and how we can raise our mind high above the earth, and commune with those divine influences: you will perceive that man is not a hurriedly put together, or an unstudied piece of work. Among her noblest products nature has none of which she can boast more than man, and assuredly no other which can comprehend her boast. What madness is this, to call the gods in question for their bounty? If a man declares that he has received nothing when he is receiving all the while, and from those who will always be giving without ever receiving anything in return, how will he be grateful to those whose kindness cannot be returned without expense? and how great a mistake is it not to be thankful to a giver, because he is good even to him who disowns him, or to use the fact of his bounty being poured upon us in an uninterrupted stream, as an argument to prove that he cannot help bestowing it. Suppose that such men as these say, "I do not want it," "Let him keep it to himself," "Who asks him for it?" and so forth, with all the other speeches of insolent minds: still, he whose bounty reaches you, although you say that it does not, lays you under an obligation nevertheless; indeed, perhaps the greatest part of the benefit which he bestows is that he is ready to give even when you are complaining against him.

XXIV. Do you not see how parents force children during their infancy to undergo what is useful for their health? Though the children cry and struggle, they swathe them and bind their limbs straight lest premature liberty should make them grow crooked, afterwards instill into them a liberal education, threatening those who are unwilling to learn, and finally, if spirited young men do not conduct themselves frugally, modestly, and respectably, they compel them to do so. Force and harsh measures are used even to youths who have grown up and are their own masters, if they, either from fear or from insolence, refuse to take what is good for them. Thus the greatest benefits that we receive, we receive either without knowing it, or against our will, from our parents.

XXV. Those persons who are ungrateful and repudiate benefits, not because they do not wish to receive them, but in order that they may not be laid under an obligation for them, are like those who fall into the opposite extreme, and are over grateful, who pray that some trouble or misfortune may befall their benefactors to give them an opportunity of proving how gratefully they remember the benefit which they have received. It is a question whether they are right, and show a truly dutiful feeling; their state of mind is morbid, like that of frantic lovers who long for their mistress to be exiled, that they may accompany her when she leaves her country forsaken by all her friends, or that she may be poor in order that she may the more need what they give her, or who long that she may be ill in order that they may sit by her bedside, and who, in short, out of sheer love form the same wishes as her enemies would wish for her. Thus the results of hatred and of frantic love are very nearly the same; and these lovers are very like those who hope that their friends may meet with difficulties which they may remove, and who thus do a wrong that they may bestow a benefit, whereas it would have been much better for them to do nothing, than by a crime to gain an opportunity of doing good service. What should we say of a pilot who prayed to the gods for dreadful storms and tempests, in order that danger might make his skill more highly esteemed? what of a general who should pray that a vast number of the enemy surround his camp, fill the ditches by a sudden charge, tear down the rampart round his panic-stricken army, and plant its hostile standards at the very gates, in order that he might gain more glory by restoring his broken ranks and shattered fortunes? All such men confer their benefits upon us by odious means, for they beg the gods to harm those whom they mean to help, and wish them to be struck down before they raise them up; it is a cruel feeling, brought about by a distorted sense of gratitude, to wish evil to befall one whom one is bound in honour to succour.

XXVI. "My wish," argues our opponent, "does him no harm, because when I wish for the danger I wish for the rescue at the same time." What you mean by this is not that you do no wrong, but that you do less than if you wished that the danger might befall him, without wishing for the rescue. It is wicked to throw a man into the water in order that you may pull him out, to throw him down that you may raise him up, or to shut him up that you may release him. You do not bestow a benefit upon a man by ceasing to wrong him, nor can it ever be a piece of good service to anyone to remove from him a burden which you yourself imposed on him. True, you may cure the hurt which you inflict, but I had rather that you did not hurt me at all. You may gain my gratitude by curing me because I am wounded, but not by wounding me in order that you may cure me: no man likes scars except as compared with wounds, which he is glad to see thus healed, though he had rather not have received them. It would be cruel to wish such things to befall one from whom you had never received a kindness; how much more cruel is it to wish that they may befall one in whose debt you are.

XXVII. "I pray," replies he, "at the same time, that I may be able to help him." In the first place, if I stop you short in the middle of your prayer, it shows at once that you are ungrateful: I have not yet heard what you wish to do for him; I have heard what you wish him to suffer. You pray that anxiety and fear and even worse evil than this may come upon him. You desire that he may need aid: this is to his disadvantage; you desire that he may need your aid: this is to your advantage. You do not wish to help him, but to be set free from your obligation to him: for when you are eager to repay your debt in such a way as this, you merely wish to be set free from the debt, not to repay it. So the only part of your wish that could be thought honourable proves to be the base and ungrateful feeling of unwillingness to lie under an obligation: for what you wish for is, not that you may have an opportunity of repaying his kindness, but that he may be forced to beg you to do him a kindness. You make yourself the superior, and you wickedly degrade beneath your feet the man who has done you good service. How much better would it be to remain in his debt in an honourable and friendly manner, than to seek to discharge the debt by these evil means! You would be less to blame if you denied that you had received it, for your benefactor would then lose nothing more than what he gave you, whereas now you wish him to be rendered inferior to you, and brought by the loss of his property and social position into a condition below his own benefits. Do you think yourself grateful? Just utter your wishes in the hearing of him to whom you wish to do good. Do you call that a prayer for his welfare, which can be divided between his friend and his enemy, which, if the last part were omitted, you would not doubt was pronounced, by one who opposed and hated him? Enemies in war have sometimes wished to capture certain towns in order to spare them, or to conquer certain persons in order to pardon, them, yet these were the wishes of enemies, and what was the kindest part of them began by cruelty. Finally, what sort of prayers do you think those can be which he, on whose behalf they are made, hopes more earnestly than any one else may not be granted? In hoping that the gods may injure a man, and that you may help him, you deal most dishonourably with him, and you do not treat the gods themselves fairly, for you give them the odious part to play, and reserve the generous one for yourself: the gods must do him wrong in order that you may do him a service. If you were to suborn an informer to accuse a man, and afterwards withdrew him, if you engaged a man in a law suit and afterwards gave it up, no one would hesitate to call you a villain: what difference does it make, whether you attempt to do this by chicanery or by prayer, unless it be that by prayer you raise up more powerful enemies to him than by the other means? You cannot say "Why, what harm do I do him?" your prayer is either futile or harmful, indeed it is harmful even though nothing comes of it. You do your friend wrong by wishing him harm: you must thank the gods that you do him no harm. The fact of your wishing it is enough: we ought to be just as angry with you as if you had effected it.

XXVIII. "If," argues our adversary, "my prayers had any efficacy, they would also have been efficacious to save him from danger." In the first place, I reply, the danger into which you wish me to fall is certain, the help which I should receive is uncertain. Or call them both certain; it is that which injures me that comes first. Besides, YOU understand the terms of your wish; I shall be tossed by the storm without being sure that I have a haven of rest at hand.

Think what torture it must have been to me, even if I receive your help, to have stood in need of it: if I escape safely, to have trembled for myself; if I be acquitted, to have had to plead my cause. To escape from fear, however great it may be, can never be so pleasant as to live in sound unassailable safety. Pray that you may return my kindnesses when I need their return, but do not pray that I may need them. You would have done what you prayed for, had it been in your power.

XXIX. How far more honourable would a prayer of this sort be: "I pray that he may remain in such a position as that he may always bestow benefits and never need them: may he be attended by the means of giving and helping, of which he makes such a bountiful use; may he never want benefits to bestow, or be sorry for any which he has bestowed; may his nature, fitted as it is for acts of pity, goodness, and clemency, be stimulated and brought out by numbers of grateful persons, whom I trust he will find without needing to make trial of their gratitude; may he refuse to be reconciled to no one, and may no one require to be reconciled to him: may fortune so uniformly continue to favour him that no one may be able to return his kindness in any way except by feeling grateful to him."

How far more proper are such prayers as these, which do not put you off to some distant opportunity, but express your gratitude at once? What is there to prevent your returning your benefactor's kindness, even while he is in prosperity? How many ways are there by which we can repay what we owe even to the affluent—for instance, by honest advice, by constant intercourse, by courteous conversation, pleasing him without flattering him, by listening attentively to any subject which he may wish to discuss, by keeping safe any secret that he may impart to us, and by social intercourse. There is no one so highly placed by fortune as not to want a friend all the more because he wants nothing.

XXX. The other is a melancholy opportunity, and one which we ought always to pray may be kept far from us: must the gods be angry with a man in order that you may prove your gratitude to him? Do you not perceive that you are doing wrong, from the very fact that those to whom you are ungrateful fare better? Call up before your mind dungeons, chains, wretchedness, slavery, war, poverty: these are the opportunities for which you pray; if any one has any dealings with you, it is by means of these that you square your account. Why not rather wish that he to whom you owe most may be powerful and happy? for, as I have just said, what is there to prevent your returning the kindness even of those who enjoy the greatest prosperity? to do which, ample and various opportunities will present themselves to you, What! do you not know that a debt can be paid even to a rich man? Nor will I trouble you with many instances of what you may do. Though a man's riches and prosperity may prevent your making him any other repayment, I will show you what the highest in the land stand in need of, what is wanting to those who possess everything. They want a man to speak the truth, to save them from the organized mass of falsehood by which they are beset, which so bewilders them with lies that the habit of hearing only what is pleasant instead of what is true, prevents their knowing what truth really is. Do you not see how such persons are driven to ruin by the want of candour among their friends, whose loyalty has degenerated into slavish obsequiousness? No one, when giving them his advice, tells them what he really thinks, but each vies with the other in flattery; and while the man's friends make it their only object to see who can most pleasantly deceive him, he himself is ignorant of his real powers, and, believing himself to be as great a man as he is told that he is, plunges the State in useless wars, which bring disasters upon it, breaks off a useful and necessary peace, and, through a passion of anger which no one checks, spills the blood of numbers of people, and at last sheds his own. Such persons assert what has never been investigated as certain facts, consider that to modify their opinion is as dishonourable as to be conquered, believe that institutions which are just flickering out of existence will last for ever, and, thus overturn great States, to the destruction of themselves and all who are connected with them. Living as they do in a fool's paradise, resplendent with unreal and short-lived advantages, they forget that, as soon as they put it out of their power to hear the truth, there is no limit to the misfortunes which they may expect.

XXXI. When Xerxes declared war against Greece, all his courtiers encouraged his boastful temper, which forgot how unsubstantial his grounds for confidence were. One declared that the Greeks would not endure to hear the news of the declaration of war, and would take to flight at the first rumour of his approach; another, that with such a vast army Greece could not only be conquered, but utterly overwhelmed, and that it was rather to be feared that they would find the Greek cities empty and abandoned, and that the panic flight of the enemy would leave them only vast deserts, where no use could be made of their enormous forces. Another told him that the world was hardly large enough to contain him, that the seas were too narrow for his fleets, the camps would not take in his armies, the plains were not wide enough to deploy his cavalry in, and that the sky itself was scarcely large enough to enable all his troops to hurl their darts at once. While much boasting of this sort was going on around him, raising his already overweening self-confidence to a frantic pitch, Demaratus, the Lacedaemonian, alone told him that the disorganized and unwieldy multitude in which he trusted, was in itself a danger to its chief, because it possessed only weight without strength; for an army which is too large cannot be governed, and one which cannot be governed, cannot long exist. "The Lacedaemonians," said he, "will meet you upon the first mountain in Greece, and will give you a taste of their quality. All these thousands of nations of yours will be held in check by three hundred men: they will stand firm at their posts, they will defend the passes entrusted to them with their weapons, and block them up with their bodies: all Asia will not force them to give way; few as they are, they will stop all this terrible invasion, attempted though it be by nearly the whole human race. Though the laws of nature may give way to you, and enable you to pass from Europe to Asia, yet you will stop short in a bypath; consider what your losses will be afterwards, when you have reckoned up the price which you have to pay for the pass of Thermopylae; when you learn that your march can be stayed, you will discover that you may be put to flight. The Greeks will yield up many parts of their country to you, as if they were swept out of them by the first terrible rush of a mountain torrent; afterwards they will rise against you from all quarters and will crush you by means of your own strength. What people say, that your warlike preparations are too great to be contained in the countries which you intend to attack, is quite true; but this is to our disadvantage. Greece will conquer you for this very reason, that she cannot contain you; you cannot make use of the whole of your force. Besides this, you will not be able to do what is essential to victory—that is, to meet the manoeuvres of the enemy at once, to support your own men if they give way, or to confirm and strengthen them when their ranks are wavering; long before you know it, you will be defeated. Moreover, you should not think that because your army is so large that its own chief does not know its numbers, it is therefore irresistible; there is nothing so great that it cannot perish; nay, without any other cause, its own excessive size may prove its ruin." What Demaratus predicted came to pass. He whose power gods and men obeyed, and who swept away all that opposed him, was bidden to halt by three hundred men, and the Persians, defeated in every part of Greece, learned how great a difference there is between a mob and an army. Thus it came to pass that Xerxes, who suffered more from the shame of his failure than from the losses which he sustained, thanked Demaratus for having been the only man who told him the truth, and permitted him to ask what boon he pleased. He asked to be allowed to drive a chariot into Sardis, the largest city in Asia, wearing a tiara erect upon his head, a privilege which was enjoyed by kings alone. He deserved his reward before he asked for it, but how wretched must the nation have been, in which there was no one who would speak the truth to the king except one man who did not speak it to himself.

XXXII. The late Emperor Augustus banished his daughter, whose conduct went beyond the shame of ordinary immodesty, and made public the scandals of the imperial house.

Led away by his passion, he divulged all these crimes which, as emperor, he ought to have kept secret with as much care as he punished them, because the shame of some deeds asperses even him who avenges them. Afterwards, when by lapse of time shame took the place of anger in his mind, he lamented that he had not kept silence about matters which he had not learned until it was disgraceful to speak of them, and often used to exclaim, "None of these things would have happened to me, if either Agrippa or Maecenas had lived!" So hard was it for the master of so many thousands of men to repair the loss of two. When his legions were slaughtered, new ones were at once enrolled; when his fleet was wrecked, within a few days another was afloat; when the public buildings were consumed by fire, finer ones arose in their stead; but the places of Agrippa and Maecenas remained unfilled throughout his life. What am I to imagine? that there were not any men like these, who could take their place, or that it was the fault of Augustus himself, who preferred mourning for them to seeking for their likes? We have no reason for supposing that it was the habit of Agrippa or Maecenas to speak the truth to him; indeed, if they had lived they would have been as great dissemblers as the rest. It is one of the habits of kings to insult their present servants by praising those whom they have lost, and to attribute the virtue of truthful speaking to those from whom there is no further risk of hearing it.

XXXIII. However, to return to my subject, you see how easy it is to return the kindness of the prosperous, and even of those who occupy the highest places of all mankind. Tell them, not what they wish to hear, but what they will wish that they always had heard; though their ears be stopped by flatteries, yet sometimes truth may penetrate them; give them useful advice. Do you ask what service you can render to a prosperous man? Teach him not to rely upon his prosperity, and to understand that it ought to be supported by the hands of many trusty friends. Will you not have done much for him, if you take away his foolish belief that his influence will endure for ever, and teach him that what we gain by chance passes away soon, and at a quicker rate than it came; that we cannot fall by the same stages by which we rose to the height of good fortune, but that frequently between it and ruin there is but one step? You do not know how great is the value of friendship, if you do not understand how much you give to him to whom you give a friend, a commodity which is scarce not only in men's houses, but in whole centuries, and which is nowhere scarcer than in the places where it is thought to be most plentiful. Pray, do you suppose that those books of names, which your nomenclator [Footnote: The nomenclator was a slave who attended his master in canvassing and on similar occasions, for the purpose of telling him the names of whom he met in the street.] can hardly carry or remember, are those of friends? It is not your friends who crowd to knock at your door, and who are admitted to your greater or lesser levees.

XXXIV. To divide one's friends into classes is an old trick of kings and their imitators; it shows great arrogance to think that to touch or to pass one's threshold can be a valuable privilege, or to grant as an honour that you should sit nearer one's front door than others, or enter house before them, although within the house there are many more doors, which shut out even those who have been admitted so far. With us Gaius Gracchus, and shortly after him Livius Drusus, were the first to keep themselves apart from the mass of their adherents, and to admit some to their privacy, some to their more select, and others to their general receptions. These men consequently had friends of the first and second rank, and so on, but in none had they true friends. Can you apply the name of friend to one who is admitted in his regular order to pay his respects to you? or can you expect perfect loyalty from one who is forced to slip into your presence through a grudgingly-opened door? How can a man arrive at using bold freedom of speech with you, if he is only allowed in his proper turn to make use of the common phrase, "Hail to you," which is used by perfect strangers? Whenever you go to any of these great men, whose levees interest the whole city, though you find all the streets beset with throngs of people, and the passers-by hardly able to make their way through the crowd, you may be sure that you have come to a place where there are many men, but no friends of their patron. We must not seek our friends in our entrance hall, but in our own breast; it is there that he ought to be received, there retained, and hoarded up in our minds. Teach this, and you will have repaid your debt of gratitude.

XXXV. If you are useful to your friend only when he is in distress, and are superfluous when all goes well with him, you form a mean estimate of your own value. As you can bear yourself wisely both in doubtful, in prosperous, and in adverse circumstances, by showing prudence in doubtful cases, courage in misfortune, and self-restraint in good fortune, so in all circumstances you can make yourself useful to your friend. Do not desert him in adversity, but do not wish that it may befall him: the various incidents of human life will afford you many opportunities of proving your loyalty to him without wishing him evil. He who prays that another may become rich, in order that he may share his riches, really has a view to his own advantage, although his prayers are ostensibly offered in behalf of his friend; and similarly he who wishes that his friend may get into some trouble from which his own friendly assistance may extricate him—a most ungrateful wish—prefers himself to his friend, and thinks it worthwhile that his friend should be unhappy, in order that he may prove his gratitude. This very wish makes him ungrateful, for he wishes to rid himself of his gratitude as though it were a heavy burden. In returning a kindness it makes a great difference whether you are eager to bestow a benefit, or merely to free yourself from a debt. He who wishes to return a benefit will study his friend's interests, and will hope that a suitable occasion will arise; he who only wishes to free himself from an obligation will be eager to do so by any means whatever, which shows very bad feeling. "Do you say," we may be asked, "that eagerness to repay kindness belongs to a morbid feeling of gratitude?" I cannot explain my meaning more clearly than by repeating what I have already said. You do not want to repay, but to escape from the benefit which you have received. You seem to say, "When shall I get free from this obligation? I must strive by any means in my power to extinguish my debt to him." You would be thought to be far from grateful, if you wished to pay a debt to him with his own money; yet this wish of yours is even more unjust; for you invoke curses upon him, and call down terrible imprecations upon the head of one who ought to be held sacred by you. No one, I suppose, would have any doubt of your wickedness if you were openly to pray that he might suffer poverty, captivity, hunger, or fear; yet what is the difference between openly praying for some of these things, and silently wishing for them? for you do wish for some of these. Go, and enjoy your belief that this is gratitude, to do what not even an ungrateful man would do, supposing he confined himself to repudiating the benefit, and did not go so far as to hate his benefactor.

XXXVI. Who would call Aeneas pious, if he wished that his native city might be captured, in order that he might save his father from captivity? Who would point to the Sicilian youths as good examples for his children, if they had prayed that Aetna might flame with unusual heat and pour forth a vast mass of fire in order to afford them an opportunity of displaying their filial affection by rescuing their parents from the midst of the conflagration? Rome owes Scipio nothing if he kept the Punic War alive in order that he might have the glory of finishing it; she owes nothing to the Decii if they prayed for public disasters, to give themselves an opportunity of displaying their brave self-devotion. It is the greatest scandal for a physician to make work for himself; and many who have aggravated the diseases of their patients that they may have the greater credit for curing them, have either failed to cure them, at all or have done so at the cost of the most terrible suffering to their victims.

XXXVII. It is said (at any rate Hecaton tells us) that when Callistratus with many others was driven into exile by his factious and licentiously free country, some one prayed that such trouble might befall the Athenians that they would be forced to recall the exiles, on hearing which, he prayed that God might forbid his return upon such terms. When some one tried to console our own countryman, Rutilius, for his exile, pointing out that civil war was at hand, and that all exiles would soon be restored to Rome, he answered with even greater spirit, "What harm have I done you, that you should wish that I may return to my country more unhappily than I quit it? My wish is, that my country should blush at my being banished, rather than that she should mourn at my having returned." An exile, of which every one is more ashamed than the sufferer, is not exile at all. These two persons, who did not wish to be restored to their homes at the cost of a public disaster, but preferred that two should suffer unjustly than that all should suffer alike, are thought to have acted like good citizens; and in like manner it does not accord with the character of a grateful man, to wish that his benefactor may fall into troubles which he may dispel; because, even though he may mean well to him, yet he wishes him evil. To put out a fire which you yourself have lighted, will not even gain acquittal for you, let alone credit.

XXXVIII. In some states an evil wish was regarded as a crime. It is certain that at Athens Demades obtained a verdict against one who sold furniture for funerals, by proving that he had prayed for great gains, which he could not obtain without the death of many persons. Yet it is a stock question whether he was rightly found guilty. Perhaps he prayed, not that he might sell his wares to many persons, but that he might sell them dear, or that he might procure what he was going to sell, cheaply. Since his business consisted of buying and selling, why should you consider his prayer to apply to one branch of it only, although he made profit from both? Besides this, you might find every one of his trade guilty, for they all wish, that is, secretly pray, as he did. You might, moreover, find a great part of the human race guilty, for who is there who does not profit by his neighbour's wants? A soldier, if he wishes for glory, must wish for war; the farmer profits by corn being dear; a large number of litigants raises the price of forensic eloquence; physicians make money by a sickly season; dealers in luxuries are made rich by the effeminacy of youth; suppose that no storms and no conflagrations injured our dwellings, the builder's trade would be at a standstill. The prayer of one man was detected, but it was just like the prayers of all other men. Do you imagine that Arruntius and Haterius, and all other professional legacy-hunters do not put up the same prayers as undertakers and grave-diggers? though the latter know not whose death it is that they wish for, while the former wish for the death of their dearest friends, from whom, on account of their intimacy, they have most hopes of inheriting a fortune. No one's life does the undertaker any harm, whereas these men starve if their friends are long about dying; they do not, therefore, merely wish for their deaths in order that they may receive what they have earned by a disgraceful servitude, but in order that they may be set free from a heavy tax. There can, therefore, be no doubt that such persons repeat with even greater earnestness the prayer for which the undertaker was condemned, for whoever is likely to profit such men by dying, does them an injury by living. Yet the wishes of all these are alike well known and unpunished. Lastly, let every man examine his own self, let him look into the secret thoughts of his heart and consider what it is that he silently hopes for; how many of his prayers he would blush to acknowledge, even to himself; how few there are which we could repeat in the presence of witnesses!

XXXIX. Yet we must not condemn every thing which we find worthy of blame, as, for instance, this wish about our friends which we have been discussing, arises from a misdirected feeling of affection, and falls into the very error which it strives to avoid, for the man is ungrateful at the very time when he hurries to prove his gratitude. He prays aloud, "May he fall into my power, may he need my influence, may not be able to be safe and respectable without my aid, may he be so unfortunate that whatever return I make to him may be regarded as a benefit." To the gods alone he adds, "May domestic treasons encompass him, which can be quelled by me alone; may some powerful and virulent enemy, some excited and armed mob, assail him; may he be set upon by a creditor or an informer."

XL. See, how just you are; you would never have wished any of these misfortunes to befall him, if he had not bestowed a benefit upon you. Not to speak of the graver guilt which you incur by returning evil for good, you distinctly do wrong in not waiting for the fitting time for each action, for it is as wrong to anticipate this as it is not to take it when it comes. A benefit ought not always to be accepted, and ought not in all cases to be returned. If you were to return it to me against my will, you would be ungrateful, how much more ungrateful are you, if you force me to wish for it? Wait patiently; why are you unwilling to let my bounty abide with you? Why do you chafe at being laid under an obligation? why, as though you were dealing with a harsh usurer, are you in such a hurry to sign and seal an equivalent bond? Why do you wish me to get into trouble? Why do you call upon the gods to ruin me? If this is your way of returning a kindness, what would you do if you were exacting repayment of a debt?

XLI. Above all, therefore, my Liberalis, let us learn to live calmly under an obligation to others, and watch for opportunities of repaying our debt without manufacturing them. Let us remember that this anxiety to seize the first opportunity of setting ourselves free shows ingratitude; for no one repays with good will that which he is unwilling to owe, and his eagerness to get it out of his hands shows that he regards it as a burden rather than as a favour. How much better and more righteous is it to bear in mind what we owe to our friends, and to offer repayment, not to obtrude it, nor to think ourselves too much indebted; because a benefit is a common bond which connects two persons. Say "I do not delay to repay your kindness to me; I hope that you will accept my gratitude cheerfully. If irresistible fate hangs over either of us, and destiny rules either that you must receive your benefit back again, or that I must receive a second benefit, why then, of us two, let him give that was wont to give. I am ready to receive it.

"'Tis not the part of Turnus to delay."

That is the spirit which I shall show whenever the time comes; in the meanwhile the gods shall be my witnesses.

XLII. I have noted in you, my Liberalis, and as it were touched with my hand a feeling of fussy anxiety not to be behindhand in doing what is your duty. This anxiety is not suitable to a grateful mind, which, on the contrary, produces the utmost confidence in oneself, and which drives away all trouble by the consciousness of real affection towards one's benefactor. To say "Take back what you gave me," is no less a reproach than to say "You are in my debt." Let this be the first privilege of a benefit, that he who bestowed it may choose the time when he will have it returned. "But I fear that men may speak ill of me." You do wrong if you are grateful only for the sake of your reputation, and not to satisfy your conscience. You have in this matter two judges, your benefactor, whom you ought not, and yourself, whom you cannot deceive. "But," say you, "if no occasion of repayment offers, am I always to remain in his debt?" Yes; but you should do so openly, and willingly, and should view with great pleasure what he has entrusted to you. If you are vexed at not having yet returned a benefit, you must be sorry that you ever received it; but if he deserved that you should receive a benefit from him, why should he not deserve that you should long remain in his debt?

XLIII. Those persons are much mistaken who regard it as a proof of a great mind to make offers to give, and to fill many men's pockets and houses with their presents, for sometimes these are due not to a great mind, but to a great fortune; they do not know how far more great and more difficult it sometimes is to receive than to lavish gifts. I must disparage neither act; it is as proper to a noble heart to owe as to receive, for both are of equal value when done virtuously; indeed, to owe is the more difficult, because it requires more pains to keep a thing safe than to give it away. We ought not therefore to be in a hurry to repay, nor need we seek to do so out of due season, for to hasten to make repayment at the wrong time is as bad as to be slow to do so at the right time. My benefactor has entrusted his bounty to me: I ought not to have any fears either on his behalf or on my own. He has a sufficient security; he cannot lose it except he loses me—nay, not even if he loses me. I have returned thanks to him for it—that is, I have requited him. He who thinks too much about repaying a benefit must suppose that his friend thinks too much about receiving repayment. Make no difficulty about either course. If he wishes to receive his benefit back again, let us return it cheerfully; if he prefers to leave it in our hands, why should we dig up his treasure? why should we decline to be its guardians? he deserves to be allowed to do whichever he pleases. As for fame and reputation, let us regard them as matters which ought to accompany, but which ought not to direct our actions.

BOOK VII.

I.

Be of good cheer, my Liberalis:

"Our port is close, and I will not delay,
 Nor by digressions wander from the way."

This book collects together all that has been omitted, and in it, having exhausted my subject, I shall consider not what I am to say, but what there is which I have not yet said. If there be anything superfluous in it, I pray you take it in good part, since it is for you that it is superfluous. Had I wished to set off my work to the best advantage, I ought to have added to it by degrees, and to have kept for the last that part which would be eagerly perused even by a sated reader. However, instead of this, I have collected together all that was essential in the beginning; I am now collecting together whatever then escaped me; nor, by Hercules, if you ask me, do I think that, after the rules which govern our conduct have been stated, it is very much to the purpose to discuss the other questions which have been raised more for the exercise of our intellects than for the health of our minds. The cynic Demetrius, who in my opinion was a great man even if compared with the greatest philosophers, had an admirable saying about this, that one gained more by having a few wise precepts ready and in common use than by learning many without having them at hand. "The best wrestler," he would say, "is not he who has learned thoroughly all the tricks and twists of the art, which are seldom met with in actual wrestling, but he who has well and carefully trained himself in one or two of them, and watches keenly for an opportunity of practising them. It does not matter how many of them he knows, if he knows enough to give him the victory; and so in this subject of ours there are many points of interest, but few of importance. You need not know what is the system of the ocean tides, why each seventh year leaves its mark upon the human body, why the more distant parts of a long portico do not keep their true proportion, but seem to approach one another until at last the spaces between the columns disappear, how it can be that twins are conceived separately, though they are born together, whether both result from one, or each from a separate act, why those whose birth was the same should have such different fates in life, and dwell at the greatest possible distance from one another, although they were born touching one another; it will not do you much harm to pass over matters which we are not permitted to know, and which we should not profit by knowing. Truths so obscure may be neglected with impunity. [Footnote: The old saying, 'Truth lurks deep in a well (or abyss).'] Nor can we complain that nature deals hardly with us, for there is nothing which is hard to discover except those things by which we gain nothing beyond the credit of having discovered them; whatever things tend to make us better or happier are either obvious or easily discovered. Your mind can rise superior to the accidents of life, if it can raise itself above fears and not greedily covet boundless wealth, but has learned to seek for riches within itself; if it has cast out the fear of men and gods, and has learned that it has not much to fear from man, and nothing to fear from God; if by scorning all those things which make life miserable while they adorn it, the mind can soar to such a height as to see clearly that death cannot be the beginning of any trouble, though it is the end of many; if it can dedicate itself to righteousness and think any path easy which leads to it; if, being a gregarious creature, and born for the common good, it regards the world as the universal home, if it keeps its conscience clear towards God and lives always as though in public, fearing itself more than other men, then it avoids all storms, it stands on firm ground in fair daylight, and has brought to perfection its knowledge of all that is useful and essential. All that remains serves merely to amuse our leisure; yet, when once anchored in safety, the mind may consider these matters also, though it can derive no strength, but only culture from their discussion."

II. The above are the rules which my friend Demetrius bids

him who would make progress in philosophy to clutch with both hands, never to let go, but to cling to them, and make them a part of himself, and by daily meditation upon them to bring himself into such a state of mind, that these wholesome maxims occur to him of their own accord, that wherever he may be, they may straightway be ready for use when required, and that the criterion of right and wrong may present itself to him without delay. Let him know that nothing is evil except what is base, and nothing good except what is honourable: let him guide his life by this rule: let him both act and expect others to act in accordance with this law, and let him regard those whose minds are steeped in indolence, and who are given up to lust and gluttony, as the most pitiable of mankind, no matter how splendid their fortunes may be. Let him say to himself, "Pleasure is uncertain, short, apt to pall upon us, and the more eagerly we indulge in it, the sooner we bring on a reaction of feeling against it; we must necessarily afterwards blush for it, or be sorry for it, there is nothing grand about it, nothing worthy of man's nature, little lower as it is than that of the gods; pleasure is a low act, brought about by the agency of our inferior and baser members, and shameful in its result. True pleasure, worthy of a human being and of a man, is, not to stuff or swell his body with food and drink, nor to excite lusts which are least hurtful when they are most quiet, but to be free from all forms of mental disturbance, both those which arise from men's ambitious struggles with one another, and those which come from on high and are more difficult to deal with, which flow from our taking the traditional view of the gods, and estimating them by the analogy of our own vices." This equable, secure, uncloying pleasure is enjoyed by the man now described; a man skilled, so to say, in the laws of gods and men alike. Such a man enjoys the present without anxiety for the future: for he who depends upon what is uncertain can rely confidently upon nothing. Thus he is free from all those great troubles which unhinge the mind, he neither hopes for, nor covets anything, and engages in no uncertain adventures, being satisfied with what he has. Do not suppose that he is satisfied with a little; for everything is his, and that not in the sense in which all was Alexander's, who, though he reached the shore of the Red Sea, yet wanted more territory than that through which he had come. He did not even own those countries which he held or had conquered, while Onesicritus, whom he had sent on before him to discover new countries, was wandering about the ocean and engaging in war in unknown seas. Is it clear that he who pushed his armies beyond the bounds of the universe, who with reckless greed dashed headlong into a boundless and unexplored sea, must in reality have been full of wants? It matters not how many kingdoms he may have seized or given away, or how great a part of the world may pay him tribute; such a man must be in need of as much as he desires.

III. This was not the vice of Alexander alone, who followed with a fortunate audacity in the footsteps of Bacchus and Hercules, but it is common to all those whose covetousness is whetted rather than appeased by good fortune. Look at Cyrus and Cambyses and all the royal house of Persia: can you find one among them who thought his empire large enough, or was not at the last gasp still aspiring after further conquests? We need not wonder at this, for whatever is obtained by covetousness is simply swallowed up and lost, nor does it matter how much is poured into its insatiable maw. Only the wise man possesses everything without having to struggle to retain it; he alone does not need to send ambassadors across the seas, measure out camps upon hostile shores, place garrisons in commanding forts, or manoeuvre legions and squadrons of cavalry. Like the immortal gods, who govern their realm without recourse to arms, and from their serene and lofty heights protect their own, so the wise man fulfils his duties, however far-reaching they may be, without disorder, and looks down upon the whole human race, because he himself is the greatest and most powerful member thereof. You may laugh at him, but if you in your mind survey the east and the west, reaching even to the regions separated from us by vast wildernesses, if you think of all the creatures of the earth, all the riches which the bounty of nature lavishes, it shows a great spirit to be able to say, as though you were a god, "All these are mine." Thus it is that he covets nothing, for there is nothing which is not contained in everything, and everything is his.

IV. "This," say you, "is the very thing that I wanted! I have caught you! I shall be glad to see how you will extricate yourself from the toils into which you have fallen of your own accord. Tell me, if the wise man possesses everything, how can one give anything to a wise man? for even what you give him is his already. It is impossible, therefore, to bestow a benefit upon a wise man, if whatever is given him comes from his own store; yet you Stoics declare that it is possible to give to a wise man. I make the same inquiry about friends as well: for you say that friends own everything in common, and if so, no one can give anything to his friend, for he gives what his friend owned already in common with himself."

There is nothing to prevent a thing belonging to a wise man, and yet being the property of its legal owner. According to law everything in a state belongs to the king, yet all that property over which the king has rights of possession is parcelled out among individual owners, and each separate thing belongs to somebody: and so one can give the king a house, a slave, or a sum of money without being said to give him what was his already; for the king has rights over all these things, while each citizen has the ownership of them. We speak of the country of the Athenians, or of the Campanians, though the inhabitants divide them amongst themselves into separate estates; the whole region belongs to one state or another, but each part of it belongs to its own individual proprietor; so that we are able to give our lands to the state, although they are reckoned as belonging to the state, because we and the state own them in different ways. Can there be any doubt that all the private savings of a slave belong to his master as well as he himself? yet he makes his master presents. The slave does not therefore possess nothing, because if his master chose he might possess nothing; nor does what he gives of his own free will cease to be a present, because it might have been wrung from him against his will. As for how we are to prove that the wise man possesses all things, we shall see afterwards; for the present we are both agreed to regard this as true; we must gather together something to answer the question before us, which is, how any means remain of acting generously towards one who already possesses all things? All things that a son has belong to his father, yet who does not know that in spite of this a son can make presents to his father? All things belong to the gods; yet we make presents and bestow alms even upon the gods. What I have is not necessarily not mine because it belongs to you; for the same thing may belong both to me and to you.

"He to whom courtezans belong," argues our adversary, "must be a procurer: now courtezans are included in all things, therefore courtezans belong to the wise man. But he to whom courtezans belong is a procurer; therefore the wise man is a procurer." Yes! by the same reasoning, our opponents would forbid him to buy anything, arguing, "No man buys his own property. Now all things are the property of the wise man; therefore the wise man buys nothing." By the same reasoning they object to his borrowing, because no one pays interest for the use of his own money. They raise endless quibbles, although they perfectly well understand what we say.

V. For, when I say that the wise man possesses everything, I mean that he does so without thereby impairing each man's individual rights in his own property, in the same way as in a country ruled by a good king, everything belongs to the king, by the right of his authority, and to the people by their several rights of ownership. This I shall prove in its proper place; in the mean time it is a sufficient answer to the question to declare that I am able to give to the wise man that which is in one way mine, and in another way his. Nor is it strange that I should be able to give anything to one who possesses everything. Suppose I have hired a house from you: some part of that house is mine, some is yours; the house itself is yours, the use of your house belongs to me. Crops may ripen upon your land, but you cannot touch them against the will of your tenant; and if corn be dear, or at famine price, you will

"In vain another's mighty store behold,"

grown upon your land, lying upon your land, and to be deposited in your own barns. Though you be the landlord, you must not enter my hired house, nor may you take away your own slave from me if I have contracted for his services; nay, if I hire a carriage from you, I bestow a benefit by allowing you to take your seat in it, although it is your own. You see, therefore, that it is possible for a man to receive a present by accepting what is his own.

VI. In all the cases which I have mentioned, each party is the owner of the same thing. How is this? It is because the one owns the thing, the other owns the use of the thing. We speak of the books of Cicero. Dorus, the bookseller, calls these same books his own; the one claims them because he wrote them, the other because he bought them; so that they may quite correctly be spoken of as belonging to either of the two, for they do belong to each, though in a different manner. Thus Titus Livius may receive as a present, or may buy his own books from Dorus. Although the wise man possesses everything, yet I can give him what I individually possess; for though, king-like, he in his mind possesses everything, yet the ownership of all things is divided among various individuals, so that he can both receive a present and owe one; can buy, or hire things. Everything belongs to Caesar; yet he has no private property beyond his own privy purse; as Emperor all things are his, but nothing is his own except what he inherits. It is possible, without treason, to discuss what is and what is not his; for even what the court may decide not to be his, from another point of view is his. In the same way the wise man in his mind possesses everything, in actual right and ownership he possesses only his own property.

VII. Bion is able to prove by argument at one time that everyone is sacrilegious, at another that no one is. When he is in a mood for casting all men down the Tarpeian rock, he says, "Whosoever touches that which belongs to the gods, and consumes it or converts it to his own uses, is sacrilegious; but all things belong to the gods, so that whatever thing any one touches belongs to them to whom all belongs; whoever, therefore, touches anything is sacrilegious." Again, when he bids men break open temples and pillage the Capitol without fear of the wrath of heaven, he declares that no one can be sacrilegious; because, whatever a man takes away, he takes from one place which belongs to the gods into another place which belongs to the gods. The answer to this is that all places do indeed belong to the gods, but all are not consecrated to them, and that sacrilege can only be done in places solemnly dedicated to heaven. Thus, also, the whole world is a temple of the immortal gods, and, indeed, the only one worthy of their greatness and splendour, and yet there is a distinction between things sacred and profane; all things which it is lawful to do under the sky and the stars are not lawful to do within consecrated walls. The sacrilegious man cannot do God any harm, for He is placed beyond his reach by His divine nature; yet he is punished because he seems to have done Him harm: his punishment is demanded by our feeling on the matter, and even by his own. In the same way, therefore, as he who carries off any sacred things is regarded as sacrilegious, although that which he stole is nevertheless within the limits of the world, so it is possible to steal from a wise man: for in that case it will be some, not of that universe which he possesses, but some of those things of which he is the acknowledged owner, and which are severally his own property, which will be stolen from him. The former of these possessions he will recognize as his own, the latter he will be unwilling, even if he be able to possess; he will say, as that Roman commander said, when, to reward his courage and good service to the state, he was assigned as much land as he could inclose in one day's ploughing. "You do not," said he, "want a citizen who wants more than is enough for one citizen." Do you not think that it required a much greater man to refuse this reward than to earn it? for many have taken away the landmarks of other men's property, but no one sets up limits to his own.

VIII. When, then, we consider that the mind of the truly wise man has power over all things and pervades all things, we cannot help declaring that everything is his, although, in the estimation of our common law, it may chance that he may be rated as possessing no property whatever. It makes a great difference whether we estimate what he owns by the greatness of his mind, or by the public register. He would pray to be delivered from that possession of everything of which you speak. I will not remind you of Socrates, Chrysippus, Zeno, and other great men, all the greater, however, because envy prevents no one from praising the ancients. But a short time ago I mentioned Demetrius, who seems to have been placed by nature in our times that he might prove that we could neither corrupt him nor be corrected by him; a man of consummate wisdom, though he himself disclaimed it, constant to the principles which he professed, of an eloquence worthy to deal with the mightiest subjects, scorning mere prettinesses and verbal niceties, but expressing with infinite spirit, the ideas which inspired it. I doubt not that he was endowed by divine providence with so pure a life and such power of speech in order that our age might neither be without a model nor a reproach. Had some god wished to give all our wealth to Demetrius on the fixed condition that he should not be permitted to give it away, I am sure that he would have refused to accept it, and would have said,

IX. "I do not intend to fasten upon my back a burden like this, of which I never can rid myself, nor do I, nimble and lightly equipped as I am, mean to hinder my progress by plunging into the deep morass of business transactions. Why do you offer to me what is the bane of all nations? I would not accept it even if I meant to give it away, for I see many things which it would not become me to give. I should like to place before my eyes the things which fascinate both kings and peoples, I wish to behold the price of your blood and your lives. First bring before me the trophies of Luxury, exhibiting them as you please, either in succession, or, which is better, in one mass. I see the shell of the tortoise, a foul and slothful brute, bought for immense sums and ornamented with the most elaborate care, the contrast of colours which is admired in it being obtained by the use of dyes resembling the natural tints. I see tables and pieces of wood valued at the price of a senator's estate, which are all the more precious, the more knots the tree has been twisted into by disease. I see crystal vessels, whose price is enhanced by their fragility, for among the ignorant the risk of losing things increases their value instead of lowering it, as it ought. I see murrhine cups, for luxury would be too cheap if men did not drink to one another out of hollow gems the wine to be afterwards thrown up again. I see more than one large pearl placed in each ear; for now our ears are trained to carry burdens, pearls are hung from them in pairs, and each pair has other single ones fastened above it. This womanish folly is not exaggerated enough for the men of our time, unless they hang two or three estates upon each ear. I see ladies' silk dresses, if those deserve to be called dresses which can neither cover their body or their shame; when wearing which, they can scarcely with a good conscience, swear that they are not naked. These are imported at a vast expense from nations unknown even to trade, in order that our matrons may show as much of their persons in public as they do to their lovers in private."

X. What are you doing, Avarice? see how many things there are whose price exceeds that of your beloved gold: all those which I have mentioned are more highly esteemed and valued. I now wish to review your wealth, those plates of gold and silver which dazzle our covetousness. By Hercules, the very earth, while she brings forth upon the surface every thing that is of use to us, has buried these, sunk them deep, and rests upon them with her whole weight, regarding them as pernicious substances, and likely to prove the ruin of mankind if brought into the light of day. I see that iron is brought out of the same dark pits as gold and silver, in order that we may lack neither the means nor the reward of murder. Thus far we have dealt with actual substances; but some forms of wealth deceive our eyes and minds alike. I see there letters of credit, promissory notes, and bonds, empty phantoms of property, ghosts of sick Avarice, with which she deceives our minds, which delight in unreal fancies; for what are these things, and what are interest, and account books, and usury, except the names of unnatural developments of human covetousness? I might complain of nature for not having hidden gold and silver deeper, for not having laid over it a weight too heavy to be removed: but what are your documents, your sale of time, your blood-sucking twelve per cent. interest? these are evils which we owe to our own will, which flow merely from our perverted habit, having nothing about them which can be seen or handled, mere dreams of empty avarice. Wretched is he who can take pleasure in the size of the audit book of his estate, in great tracts of land cultivated by slaves in chains, in huge flocks and herds which require provinces and kingdoms for their pasture ground, in a household of servants, more in number than some of the most warlike nations, or in a private house whose extent surpasses that of a large city! After he has carefully reviewed all his wealth, in what it is invested, and on what it is spent, and has rendered himself proud by the thoughts of it, let him compare what he has with what he wants: he becomes a poor man at once. "Let me go: restore me to those riches of mine. I know the kingdom of wisdom, which is great and stable: I possess every thing, and in such a manner that it belongs to all men nevertheless."

XI. When, therefore, Gaius Caesar offered him two hundred thousand sesterces, he laughingly refused it, thinking it unworthy of himself to boast of having refused so small a sum. Ye gods and goddesses, what a mean mind must the emperor have had, if he hoped either to honour or to corrupt him. I must here repeat a proof of his magnanimity. I have heard that when he was expressing his wonder at the folly of Gaius at supposing that he could be influenced by such a bribe, he said, "If he meant to tempt me, he ought to have tried to do so by offering his entire kingdom."

XII. It is possible, then, to give something to the wise man, although all things belong to the wise man. Similarly, though we declare that friends have all things in common, it is nevertheless possible to give something to a friend: for I have not everything in common with a friend in the same manner as with a partner, where one part belongs to him, and another to me, but rather as a father and a mother possess their children in common when they have two, not each parent possessing one child, but each possessing both. First of all I will prove that any chance would-be partner of mine has nothing in common with me: and why? Because this community of goods can only exist between wise men, who are alone capable of friendship: other men can neither be friends nor partners one to another. In the next place, things may be owned in common in various ways. The knights' seats in the theatre belong to all the Roman knights; yet of these the seat which I occupy becomes my own, and if I yield it up to any one, although I only yield him a thing which we own in common, still I appear to have given him something. Some things belong to certain persons under particular conditions. I have a place among the knights, not to sell, or to let, or to dwell in, but simply to see the spectacle from, wherefore I do not tell an untruth when I say that I have a place among the knights' seats. Yet if, when I come into the theatre, the knights' seats are full, I both have a seat there by right, because I have the privilege of sitting there, and I have not a seat there, because my seat is occupied by those who share my right to those places. Suppose that the same thing takes place between friends; whatever our friend possesses, is common to us, but is the property of him who owns it; I cannot make use of it against his will. "You are laughing at me," say you; "if what belongs to my friend is mine, I am able to sell it." You are not able; for you are not able to sell your place among the knights' seats, and yet they are in common between you and the other knights. Consequently, the fact that you cannot sell a thing, or consume it, or exchange it for the better or the worse does not prove that it is not yours; for that which is yours under certain conditions is yours nevertheless.

XIII. I have received, but certainly not less. Not to detain you longer than is necessary, a benefit can be no more than a benefit;

but the means employed to convey benefits may be both greater and more numerous. I mean those things by which kindness expresses and gives vent to itself, like lovers, whose many kisses and close embraces do not increase their love but give it play.

XIV. The next question which arises has been thoroughly threshed out in the former books, so here it shall only be touched on shortly; for the arguments which have been used for other cases can be transferred to it.

The question is, whether one who has done everything in his power to return a benefit, has returned it. "You may know," says our adversary, "that he has not returned it, because he did everything in his power to return it; it is evident, therefore, that he did not not do that which he did not have an opportunity of doing. A man who searches everywhere for his creditor without finding him does not thereby pay him what he owes." Some are in such a position that it is their duty to effect something material; in the case of others to have done all in their power to effect it is as good as effecting it. If a physician has done all in his power to heal his patient he has performed his duty; an advocate who employs his whole powers of eloquence on his client's behalf, performs his duty even though his client be convicted; the generalship even of a beaten commander is praised if he has prudently, laboriously, and courageously exercised his functions. Your friend has done all in his power to return your kindness, but your good fortune stood in his way; no adversity befell you in which he could prove the truth of his friendship; he could not give you money when you were rich, or nurse you when you were in health, or help you when you were succeeding; yet he repaid your kindness, even though you did not receive a benefit from him. Moreover, this man, being always eager, and on the watch for an opportunity of doing this, as he has expended much anxiety and much trouble upon it, has really done more than he who quickly had an opportunity of repaying your kindness. The case of a debtor is not the same, for it is not enough for him to have tried to find the money unless he pays it; in his case a harsh creditor stands over him who will not let a single day pass without charging him interest; in yours there is a most kind friend, who seeing you busy, troubled, and anxious would say.

"'Dismiss this trouble from thy breast;'

leave off disturbing yourself; I have received from you all

that I wish; you wrong me, if you suppose that I want anything further; you have fully repaid me in intention."

"Tell me," says our adversary, "if he had repaid the benefit you would say that he had returned your kindness: is, then, he who repays it in the same position as he who does not repay it?"

On the other hand, consider this: if he had forgotten the benefit which he had received, if he had not even attempted to be grateful, you would say that he had not returned the kindness; but this man has laboured day and night to the neglect of all his other duties in his devoted care to let no opportunity of proving his gratitude escape him; is then he who took no pains to return a kindness to be classed with this man who never ceased to take pains? you are unjust, if you require a material payment from me when you see that I am not wanting in intention.

XV. In short, suppose that when you are taken captive, I have borrowed money, made over my property as security to my creditor, that I have sailed in a stormy winter season along coasts swarming with pirates, that I have braved all the perils which necessarily attend a voyage even on a peaceful sea, that I have wandered through all wildernesses seeking for those men whom all others flee from, and that when I have at length reached the pirates, someone else has already ransomed you: will you say that I have not returned your kindness? Even if during this voyage I have lost by shipwreck the money that I had raised to save you, even if I myself have fallen into the prison from which I sought to release you, will you say that I have not returned your kindness? No, by Hercules! the Athenians call Harmodius and Aristogiton, tyrannicides; the hand of Mucius which he left on the enemy's altar was equivalent to the death of Porsena, and valour struggling against fortune is always illustrious, even if it falls short of accomplishing its design. He who watches each opportunity as it passes, and tries to avail himself of one after another, does more to show his gratitude than he whom the first opportunity enabled to be grateful without any trouble whatever. "But," says our adversary, "he gave you two things, material help and kindly feeling; you, therefore, owe him two." You might justly say this to one who returns your kindly feeling without troubling himself further; this man is really in your debt; but you cannot say so of one who wishes to repay you, who struggles and leaves no stone unturned to do so; for, as far as in him lies, he repays you in both kinds; in the next place, counting is not always a true test, sometimes one thing is equivalent to two; consequently so intense and ardent a wish to repay takes the place of a material repayment. Indeed, if a feeling of gratitude has no value in repaying a kindness without giving something material, then no one can be grateful to the gods, whom we can repay by gratitude alone. "We cannot," says our adversary, "give the gods anything else." Well, but if I am not able to give this man, whose kindness I am bound to return, anything beside my gratitude, why should that which is all that I can bestow on a god be insufficient to prove my gratitude towards a man?

XVI. If, however, you ask me what I really think, and wish me to give a definite answer, I should say that the one party ought to consider his benefit to have been returned, while the other ought to feel that he has not returned it; the one should release his friend from the debt, the other should hold himself bound to pay it; the one should say, "I have received;" the other should answer, "I owe." In our whole investigation, we ought to look entirely to the public good; we ought to prevent the ungrateful having any excuses in which they can take refuge, and under cover of which they can disown their debts. "I have done all in my power," say you. Well, keep on doing so still. Do you suppose that our ancestors were so foolish, as not to understand that it is most unjust that the man who has wasted the money which he received from his creditor on debauchery, or gambling, should be classed with one who lost his own property as well as that of others in a fire, by robbery, or some sadder mischance? They would take no excuse, that men might understand that they were always bound to keep their word; it was thought better that even a good excuse should not be accepted from a few persons, than that all men should be led to try to make excuses. You say that you have done all in your power to repay your debt; this ought to be enough for your friend, but not enough for you. He to whom you owe a kindness, is unworthy of gratitude if he lets all your anxious care and trouble to repay it go for nothing; and so, too, if your friend takes your good will as a repayment, you are ungrateful if you are not all the more eager to feel the obligation of the debt which he has forgiven you. Do not snap up his receipt, or call witnesses to prove it; rather seek opportunities for repaying not less than before; repay the one man because he asks for repayment, the other because he forgives you your debt; the one because he is good, the other because he is bad. You, need not, therefore, think that you have anything to do with the question whether a man be bound to repay the benefit which he has received from a wise man, if that man has ceased to be wise and has turned into a bad man. You would return a deposit which you had received from a wise man; you would return a loan even to a bad man; what grounds have you for not returning a benefit also? Because he has changed, ought he to change you? What? if you had received anything from a man when healthy, would you not return it to him when he was sick, though we always are more bound to treat our friends with more kindness when they are ailing? So, too, this man is sick in his mind; we ought to help him, and bear with him; folly is a disease of the mind.

XVII. I think here we ought to make a distinction, in order to render this point more intelligible. Benefits are of two kinds: one, the perfect and true benefit, which can only be bestowed by one wise man upon another; the other, the common vulgar form which ignorant men like ourselves interchange. With regard to the latter, there is no doubt that it is my duty to repay it whether my friend turns out to be a murderer, a thief, or an adulterer. Crimes have laws to punish them; criminals are better reformed by judges than by ingratitude; a man ought not to make you bad by being so himself. I will fling a benefit back to a bad man, I will return it to a good man; I do so to the latter, because I owe it to him; to the former, that I may not be in his debt.

XVIII. With regard to the other class of benefit, the question arises whether if I was not able to take it without being a wise man, I am able to return it, except to a wise man. For suppose I do return it to him, he cannot receive it, he is not any longer able to receive such a thing, he has lost the knowledge of how to use it. You would not bid me throw back [Footnote: i.e. in the game of ball.] a ball to a man who has lost his hand; it is folly to give any one what he cannot receive. If I am to begin to reply to the last argument, I say that I should not give him what he is unable to take; but I would return it, even though he is not able to receive it. I cannot lay him under an obligation unless he takes my bounty; but by returning it I can free myself from my obligations to him. You say, "he will not be able to use it." Let him see to that; the fault will lie with him, not with me.

XIX. "To return a thing," says our adversary, "is to hand it over to one who can receive it. Why, if you owed some wine to any man, and he bade you pour it into a net or a sieve, would you say that you had returned it? or would you be willing to return it in such a way that in the act of returning it was lost between you?" To return is to give that which you owe back to its owner when he wishes for it. It is not my duty to perform more than this; that he should possess what he has received from me is a matter for further consideration; I do not owe him the safe-keeping of his property, but the honourable payment of my debt, and it is much better that he should not have it, than that I should not return it to him. I would repay my creditor, even though he would at once take what I paid him to the market; even if he deputed an adulteress to receive the money from me, I would pay it to her; even if he were to pour the coins which he receives into a loose fold of his cloak, I would pay it. It is my business to return it to him, not to keep it and save it for him after I have returned it; I am bound to take care of his bounty when I have received it, but not when I have returned it to him. While it remains with me, it must be kept safe; but when he asks for it again I must give it to him, even though it slips out of his hands as he takes it. I will repay a good man when it is convenient; I will repay a bad man when he asks me to do so.

"You cannot," argues our adversary, "return him a benefit of the same kind as that which you received; for you received it from a wise man, and you are returning it to a fool." Do I not return to him such a benefit, as he is now able to receive? It is not my fault if I return it to him worse than I received it, the fault lies with him, and so, unless he regains his former wisdom, I shall return it in such a form as he in his fallen condition is able to receive. "But what," asks he, "if he become not only bad, but savage and ferocious, like Apollodorus or Phalaris, would you return even to such a man as this a benefit which you had received from him?" I answer, Nature does not admit of so great a change in a wise man. Men do not change from the best to the worst; even in becoming bad, he would necessarily retain some traces of goodness; virtue is never so utterly quenched as not to imprint on the mind marks which no degradation can efface. If wild animals bred in captivity escape into the woods, they still retain something of their original tameness, and are as remote from the gentlest in the one extreme as they are in the other from those which have always been wild, and have never endured to be touched by man's hand. No one who has ever applied himself to philosophy ever becomes completely wicked; his mind becomes so deeply coloured with it, that its tints can never be entirely spoiled and blackened. In the next place, I ask whether this man of yours be ferocious merely in intent, or whether he breaks out into actual outrages upon mankind? You have instanced the tyrants Apollodorus and Phalaris; if the bad man restrains their evil likeness within himself, why should I not return his benefit to him, in order to set myself free from any further dealings with him? If, however, he not only delights in human blood, but feeds upon it; if he exercises his insatiable cruelty in the torture of persons of all ages, and his fury is not prompted by anger, but by a sort of delight in cruelty, if he cuts the throats of children before the eyes of their parents; if, not satisfied with merely killing his victims, he tortures them, and not only burns but actually roasts them; if his castle is always wet with freshly shed blood; then it is not enough not to return his benefits. All connexion between me and such a man has been broken off by his destruction of the bonds of human society. If he had bestowed something upon me, but were to invade my native country, he would have lost all claim to my gratitude, and it would be counted a crime to make him any return; if he does not attack my country, but is the scourge of his own; if he has nothing to do with my nation, but torments and cuts to pieces his own, then in the same manner such depravity, though it does not render him my personal enemy, yet renders him hateful to me, and the duty which I owe to the human race is anterior to and more important than that which I owe to him as an individual.

XX. However, although this be so, and although I am freed from all obligation towards him, from the moment when, by outraging all laws, he rendered it impossible for any man to do him a wrong, nevertheless, I think I ought to make the following distinction in dealing with him. If my repayment of his benefit will neither increase nor maintain his powers of doing mischief to mankind, and is of such a character that I can return it to him without disadvantage to the public, I would return it: for instance, I would save the life of his infant child; for what harm can this benefit do to any of those who suffer from his cruelty?

But I would not furnish him with money to pay his bodyguard. If he wishes for marbles, or fine clothes, the trappings of his luxury will harm no one; but with soldiers and arms I would not furnish him. If he demands, as a great boon, actors and courtesans and such things as will soften his savage nature, I would willingly bestow them upon him. I would not furnish him with triremes and brass-beaked ships of war, but I would send him fast sailing and luxuriously-fitted vessels, and all the toys of kings who take their pleasure on the sea. If his health was altogether despaired of, I would by the same act bestow a benefit on all men and return one to him; seeing that for such characters death is the only remedy, and that he who never will return to himself, had best leave himself. However, such wickedness as this is uncommon, and is always regarded as a portent, as when the earth opens, or when fires break forth from caves under the sea; so let us leave it, and speak of those vices which we can hate without shuddering at them. As for the ordinary bad man, whom I can find in the marketplace of any town, who is feared only by individuals, I would return to him a benefit which I had received from him. It is not right that I should profit by his wickedness; let me return what is not mine to its owner. Whether he be good or bad makes no difference; but I would consider the matter most carefully, if I were not returning but bestowing it.

XXI. This point requires to be illustrated by a story. A certain Pythagoraean bought a fine pair of shoes from a shoemaker; and as they were an expensive piece of work, he did not pay ready money for them. Some time afterwards he came to the shop to pay for them, and after he had long been knocking at the closed door, some one said to him, "Why do you waste your time? The shoemaker whom you seek has been carried out of his house and buried; this is a grief to us who lose our friends for ever, but by no means so to you, who know that he will be born again," jeering at the Pythagoraean. Upon this our philosopher not unwillingly carried his three or four denarii home again, shaking them every now and then; afterwards, blaming himself for the pleasure which he had secretly felt at not paying his debt, and perceiving that he enjoyed having made this trifling gain, he returned to the shop, and saying, "the man lives for you, pay him what you owe," he passed four denarii into the shop through the crack of the closed door, and let them fall inside, punishing himself for his unconscionable greediness that he might not form the habit of appropriating that which is not his own.

XXII. If you owe anything, seek for some one to whom you may repay it, and if no one demands it, dun your own self; whether the man be good or bad is no concern of yours; repay him, and then blame him. You have forgotten, how your several duties are divided: it is right for him to forget it, but we have bidden you bear it in mind. When, however, we say that he who bestows a benefit ought to forget it, it is a mistake to suppose that we rob him of all recollection of the business, though it is most creditable to him; some of our precepts are stated over strictly in order to reduce them to their true proportions. When we say that he ought not to remember it, we mean he ought not to speak publicly, or boast of it offensively. There are some, who, when they have bestowed a benefit, tell it in all societies, talk of it when sober, cannot be silent about it when drunk, force it upon strangers, and communicate it to friends; it is to quell this excessive and reproachful consciousness that we bid him who gave it forget it, and by commanding him to do this, which is more than he is able, encourage him to keep silence.

XXIII. When you distrust those whom you order to do anything, you ought to command them to do more than enough in order that they may do what is enough. The purpose of all exaggeration is to arrive at the truth by falsehood. Consequently, he who spoke of horses as being:

"Whiter than snows and swifter than the winds,"

said what could not possibly be in order that they might be thought to be as much so as possible. And he who said:

"More firm than crags, more headlong than the stream,"

did not suppose that he should make any one believe that a man could ever be as firm as a crag. Exaggeration never hopes all its daring flights to be believed, but affirms what is incredible, that thereby it may convey what is credible. When we say, "let the man who has bestowed a benefit, forget it," what we mean is, "let him be as though he had forgotten it; let not his remembrance of it appear or be seen." When we say that repayment of a benefit ought not to be demanded, we do not utterly forbid its being demanded; for repayment must often be extorted from bad men, and even good men require to be reminded of it. Am I not to point out a means of repayment to one who does not perceive it? Am I not to explain my wants to one does not know them? Why should he (if a bad man) have the excuse, or (if a good man) have the sorrow of not knowing them? Men ought sometimes to be reminded of their debts, though with modesty, not in the tone of one demanding a legal right.

XXIV. Socrates once said in the hearing of his friends: "I would have bought a cloak, if I had had the money for it." He asked no one for money, but he reminded them all to give it. There was a rivalry between them, as to who should give it; and how should there not be? Was it not a small thing which Socrates received? Yes, but it was a great thing to be the man from whom Socrates received it. Could he blame them more gently? "I would," said he, "have bought a cloak if I had had the money for it." After this, however eager any one was to give, he gave too late; for he had already been wanting in his duty to Socrates. Because some men harshly demand repayment of debts, we forbid it, not in order that it may never be done, but that it may be done sparingly.

XXV. Aristippus once, when enjoying a perfume, said: "Bad luck to those effeminate persons who have brought so nice a thing into disrepute." We also may say, "Bad luck to those base extortioners who pester us for a fourfold return of their benefits, and have brought into disrepute so nice a thing as reminding our friends of their duty." I shall nevertheless make use of this right of friendship, and I shall demand the return of a benefit from any man from whom I would not have scrupled to ask for one, such a man as would regard the power of returning a benefit as equivalent to receiving a second one. Never, not even when complaining of him, would I say,

"A wretch forlorn upon the shore he lay,
His ship, his comrades, all were swept away;
Fool that I was, I pitied his despair,
And even gave him of my realm a share."

This is not to remind, but to reproach; this is to make one's benefits odious, to enable him, or even to make him wish to be ungrateful. It is enough, and more than enough, to remind him of it gently and familiarly:

"If aught of mine hath e'er deserved thy thanks."

To this his answer would be, "Of course you have deserved my thanks; you took me up, 'a wretch forlorn upon the shore.'"

XXVI. "But," says our adversary, "suppose that we gain nothing by this; suppose that he pretends that he has forgotten it, what ought I to do?" You now ask a very necessary question, and one which fitly concludes this branch of the subject, how, namely, one ought to bear with the ungrateful. I answer, calmly, gently, magnanimously. Never let any one's discourtesy, forgetfulness, or ingratitude, enrage you so much that you do not feel any pleasure at having bestowed a benefit upon him; never let your wrongs drive you into saying, "I wish I had not done it." You ought to take pleasure even in the ill-success of your benefit; he will always be sorry for it, even though you are not even now sorry for it. You ought not to be indignant, as if something strange had happened; you ought rather to be surprised if it had not happened. Some are prevented by difficulties, some by expense, and some by danger from returning your bounty; some are hindered by a false shame, because by returning it, they would confess that they had received it; with others ignorance of their duty, indolence, or excess of business, stands in the way. Reflect upon the insatiability of men's desires. You need not be surprised if no one repays you in a world in which no one ever gains enough. What man is there of so firm and trustworthy a mind that you can safely invest your benefits in him? One man is crazed with lust, another is the slave of his belly, another gives his whole soul to gain, caring nothing for the means by which he amasses it; some men's minds are disturbed by envy, some blinded by ambition till they are ready to fling themselves on the sword's point. In addition to this, one must reckon sluggishness of mind and old age; and also the opposites of these, restlessness and disturbance of mind, also excessive self-esteem and pride in the very things for which a man ought to be despised. I need not mention obstinate persistence in wrong-doing, or frivolity which cannot remain constant to one point; besides all this, there is headlong rashness, there is timidity which never gives us trustworthy counsel, and the numberless errors with which we struggle, the rashness of the most cowardly, the quarrels of our best friends, and that most common evil of trusting in what is most uncertain, and of undervaluing, when we have obtained it, that which we once never hoped to possess. Amidst all these restless passions, how can you hope to find a thing so full of rest as good faith?

XXVII. If a true picture of our life were to rise before your mental vision, you would, I think, behold a scene like that of a town just taken by storm, where decency and righteousness were no longer regarded, and no advice is heard but that of force, as if universal confusion were the word of command. Neither fire nor sword are spared; crime is unpunished by the laws; even religion, which saves the lives of suppliants in the very midst of armed enemies, does not check those who are rushing to secure plunder. Some men rob private houses, some public buildings; all places, sacred or profane, are alike stripped; some burst their way in, others climb over; some open a wider path for themselves by overthrowing the walls that keep them out, and make their way to their booty over ruins; some ravage without murdering, others brandish spoils dripping with their owner's blood; everyone carries off his neighbours' goods. In this greedy struggle of the human race surely you forget the common lot of all mankind, if you seek among these robbers for one who will return what he has got. If you are indignant at men being ungrateful, you ought also to be indignant at their being luxurious, avaricious and lustful; you might as well be indignant with sick men for being ugly, or with old men for being pale. It is, indeed, a serious vice, it is not to be borne, and sets men at variance with one another; nay, it rends and destroys that union by which alone our human weakness can be supported; yet it is so absolutely universal, that even those who complain of it most are not themselves free from it.

XXVIII. Consider within yourself, whether you have always shown gratitude to those to whom you owe it, whether no one's kindness has ever been wasted upon you, whether you constantly bear in mind all the benefits which you have received. You will find that those which you received as a boy were forgotten before you became a man; that those bestowed upon you as a young man slipped from your memory when you became an old one. Some we have lost, some we have thrown away, some have by degrees passed out of our sight, to some we have wilfully shut our eyes. If I am to make excuses for your weakness, I must say in the first place that human memory is a frail vessel, and is not large enough to contain the mass of things placed in it; the more it receives, the more it must necessarily lose; the oldest things in it give way to the newest. Thus it comes to pass that your nurse has hardly any influence with you, because the lapse of time has set the kindness which you received from her at so great a distance; thus it is that you no longer look upon your teacher with respect; and that now when you are busy about your candidature for the consulate or the priesthood, you forget those who supported you in your election to the quaestorship. If you carefully examine yourself, perhaps you will find the vice of which you complain in your own bosom; you are wrong in being angry with a universal failing, and foolish also, for it is your own as well; you must pardon others, that you may yourself be acquitted. You will make your friend a better man by bearing with him, you will in all cases make him a worse one by reproaching him. You can have no reason for rendering him shameless; let him preserve any remnants of modesty which he may have. Too loud reproaches have often dispelled a modesty which might have borne good fruit. No man fears to be that which all men see that he is; when his fault is made public, he loses his sense of shame.

XXIX. You say, "I have lost the benefit which I bestowed." Yet do we say that we have lost what we consecrate to heaven, and a benefit well bestowed, even though we get an ill return for it, is to be reckoned among things consecrated. Our friend is not such a man as we hoped he was; still, let us, unlike him, remain the same as we were. The loss did not take place when he proved himself so; his ingratitude cannot be made public without reflecting some shame upon us, since to complain of the loss of a benefit is a sign that it was not well bestowed. As far as we are able we ought to plead with ourselves on his behalf: "Perhaps he was not able to return it, perhaps he did not know of it, perhaps he will still do so." A wise and forbearing creditor prevents the loss of some debts by encouraging his debtor and giving him time. We ought to do the same, we ought to deal tenderly with a weakly sense of honour.

XXX. "I have lost," say you, "the benefit which I bestowed." You are a fool, and do not understand when your loss took place; you have indeed lost it, but you did so when you gave it, the fact has only now come to light. Even in the case of those benefits which appear to be lost, gentleness will do much good; the wounds of the mind ought to be handled as tenderly as those of the body. The string, which might be disentangled by patience, is often broken by a rough pull. What is the use of abuse, or of complaints? why do you overwhelm him with reproaches? why do you set him free from his obligation? even if he be ungrateful he owes you nothing after this. What sense is there in exasperating a man on whom you have conferred great favours, so as out of a doubtful friend to make a certain enemy, and one, too, who will seek to support his own cause by defaming you, or to make men say, "I do not know what the reason is that he cannot endure a man to whom he owes so much; there must be something in the background?" Any man can asperse, even if he does not permanently stain the reputation of his betters by complaining of them; nor will any one be satisfied with imputing small crimes to them, when it is only by the enormity of his falsehood that he can hope to be believed.

XXXI. What a much better way is that by which the semblance of friendship, and, indeed, if the other regains to his right mind, friendship itself is preserved! Bad men are overcome by unwearying goodness, nor does any one receive kindness in so harsh and hostile a spirit as not to love good men even while he does them wrong, when they lay him under the additional obligation of requiring no return for their kindness. Reflect, then, upon this: you say, "My kindness has met with no return, what am I to do? I ought to imitate the gods, those noblest disposers of all events, who begin to bestow their benefits on those who know them not, and persist in bestowing them on those who are ungrateful for them. Some reproach them with neglect of us, some with injustice towards us; others place them outside of their own world, in sloth and indifference, without light, and without any functions; others declare that the sun itself, to whom we owe the division of our times of labour and of rest, by whose means we are saved from being plunged in the darkness of eternal night; who, by his circuit, orders the seasons of the year, gives strength to our bodies, brings forth our crops and ripens our fruits, is merely a mass of stone, or a fortuitous collection of fiery particles, or anything rather than a god. Yet, nevertheless, like the kindest of parents, who only smile at the spiteful words of their children, the gods do not cease to heap benefits upon those who doubt from what source their benefits are derived, but continue impartially distributing their bounty among all the peoples and nations of the earth. Possessing only the power of doing good, they moisten the land with seasonable showers, they put the seas in movement by the winds, they mark time by the course of the constellations, they temper the extremes of heat and cold, of summer and winter, by breathing a milder air upon us; and they graciously and serenely bear with the faults of our erring spirits. Let us follow their example; let us give, even if much be given to no purpose, let us, in spite of this, give to others; nay, even to those upon whom our bounty has been wasted. No one is prevented by the fall of a house from building another; when one home has been destroyed by fire, we lay the foundations of another before the site has had time to cool; we rebuild ruined cities more than once upon the same spots, so untiring are our hopes of success. Men would undertake no works either on land or sea if they were not willing to try again what they have failed in once."

XXXII. Suppose a man is ungrateful, he does not injure me, but himself; I had the enjoyment of my benefit when I bestowed it upon him. Because he is ungrateful, I shall not be slower to give but more careful; what I have lost with him, I shall receive back from others. But I will bestow a second benefit upon this man himself, and will overcome him even as a good husbandman overcomes the sterility of the soil by care and culture; if I do not do so my benefit is lost to me, and he is lost to mankind. It is no proof of a great mind to give and to throw away one's bounty; the true test of a great mind is to throw away one's bounty and still to give.

www.ingramcontent.com/pod-product-compliance
Lightning Source LLC
Chambersburg PA
CBHW032254150426
43195CB00008BA/449